Judaism and Vegetarianism

Judaism and Vegetarianism

Richard H. Schwartz, Ph.D.

Exposition Press   *Smithtown, New York*

Quotations from *The Holy Scriptures* are used through the courtesy of The Jewish Publication Society of America.

First Edition

© 1982 by Richard Schwartz

Library of Congress Catalog Card Number: 81-90732

ISBN 0-682-49827-0 (hardcover)
ISBN 0-682-49828-9 (paperback)

Printed in the United States of America

In loving memory of
Bessie and Edward Susskind
whose guidance and devotion were always an inspiration

Contents

And God said: "Behold, I have given you every herb yielding seed which is upon the face of all the earth, and every tree, in which is the fruit of a tree yielding seed—to you it shall be for food."

(Genesis 1:29)

Foreword

There was a time when Mennaseh reigned in the ancient kingdom of Judah, when the Torah was forgotten in its entirety, and when the people worshiped Baal. Then an ancient scroll of the Law was discovered in the neglected Temple. During the many centuries that followed, parts of the Torah have always been sadly neglected or forgotten, although the writings remained intact.

The practice of vegetarianism is implicit in the teachings of Judaism and is evident from the oft-repeated phrase in Genesis "to man and all creatures wherein there is a living soul." This indicates a common life and a shared destiny and the principle is exemplified throughout biblical writings. Nowhere is it stated that abundance of flesh shall be the reward for observing the Law; rather, there are promises of fruits of the vine and pomegranates, wheat, barley and oil, and peace, when each man shall sit under the shade of his own fig tree, not, let it be noted, under the shadow of his own slaughterhouse.

In recent centuries the section of the Torah that has been almost completely ignored or forgotten is *tsa'ar ba'alei chayim* (the mandate to avoid cruelty to animals). True, it is still recited and often some form of observance is retained, but it is an empty husk, a pallid interpretation of a beautiful script. It is like a great actor strutting on the stage of time who has forgotten the part he was intended to play.

Recently the cataclysm of two world wars and the progress of science has metamorphasized people's minds. They now conduct a global war against Creation while giving lip service to spiritual beliefs. They use the latest developments in technology to subjugate their fellow creatures in support of the meat industry. They suppress emotions, sensitivity, and basic rights of domestic animals and reduce their status to the level of commercial, inanimate merchandise.

Nevertheless, on the horizon, a faint light appears, and slowly public opinion is awakening to the enormity of the crime being committed. The Jewish people, bearing the yoke of the Law, should be in the forefront of a worldwide campaign to halt, at least, the cruelty of the factory farms.

With this growing awareness, the time is most opportune for the appearance of this volume, and Professor Schwartz, by reason of his training and past work, patience, energy, and idealism, is eminently suited to be its author. He has taken every possible opportunity for consultation and explored every avenue for research. The result is a classic work of reference that will assist and guide all those who love Judaism and indeed all seekers after truth, so that they may follow in the footsteps of the many Orthodox Jewish leaders (including three chief rabbis) by discontinuing the obsolete practice of flesh eating. Because almost all of this flesh is produced in the factory farms by unbelievably cruel methods and because these creatures are riddled with antibiotics and sex-change hormones while alive, *kashrut* can only be truly observed by abstaining therefrom.

May the efforts of the author be blessed with success and may this book be proudly borne aloft on eagles' wings to the far corners of the earth. The author will be rewarded with the knowledge that by his efforts he will bring a step nearer the biblical prophecy that "Israel shall become a blessing unto the nations."

PHILIP L. PICK
Honorary Life President
Jewish Vegetarian Society
Editor, *The Jewish Vegetarian*

Preface

Judaism and vegetarianism? Can the two be related? After all, what is a *simcha* (Jewish celebration) or holiday dinner without gefilte fish, chopped liver, *cholent,* roast beef, chicken, and chicken soup? And what about passages in the Torah referring to Temple sacrifices of animals and the consumption of meat?

Because of these factors, this book is the result of a leap of faith, an intuition that a religion that has such powerful teachings on having compassion for animals, preserving health, feeding the hungry, helping the poor, and conserving resources must be consistent with vegetarianism. As I probed for appropriate Jewish teachings and concepts, I became increasingly convinced that to be more completely involved with the glorious goals and values of Judaism, one should be a vegetarian.

While Judaism emphasizes *tsa'ar ba'alei chayim,* compassion for animals, animals are raised for food today under cruel conditions, in crowded, confined cells, where they are denied fresh air, exercise, and any emotional stimulation.

While Judaism mandates that we be very careful about preserving our health and our lives, flesh-centered diets have been linked to heart disease, several forms of cancer, and other illnesses.

While Judaism stresses that we are to share our bread with the hungry, over 80 percent of grains grown in the United States and other developed countries is fed to animals destined for slaughter, as millions die annually because of hunger and its effects.

While Judaism teaches that "the earth is the Lord's" and we

are partners with God in preserving the world and seeing that the earth's resources are properly used, a flesh-centered diet requires the wasteful use of food and other resources, and results in much pollution.

While Judaism stresses that we must seek and pursue peace and that violence results from unjust conditions, flesh-centered diets, by wasting valuable resources, help to perpetuate the widespread hunger and poverty that eventually lead to instability and war.

There are many indications in the Jewish tradition that point toward vegetarianism. The first dietary law (Gen. 1:29) allowed only vegetarian foods. When permission to eat meat was given, as a concession to people's weakness, many prohibitions and restrictions were applied to keep alive a sense of reverence for life. After the Exodus of the Children of Israel from Egypt, a second nonflesh diet was attempted in the form of manna. When the Israelites cried out for meat, God was angry. He finally relented and provided meat, but a plague broke out and many Jews died. According to Rabbi Abraham Kook, the first chief rabbi of the prestate of Israel, based on the prophecy of Isaiah (". . . the lion will eat straw like the ox. . . ."), people will again be vegetarians in the time of the Messiah.

Many difficult questions are asked of vegetarians who take the Jewish tradition seriously. These include: Don't we have to eat meat on the Sabbath and to celebrate joyous events? Isn't it a sin not to take advantage of pleasurable things like eating meat? Weren't we given dominion over animals? What about sacrificial Temple services? These and other questions will be considered. In addition, a chapter on nutrition has been contributed by Shoshana Margolin, N.D., H.M.D., to ease the way into the world of healthful vegetarian eating.

There have been several recent examples of increased Jewish interest and involvement in vegetarianism. Jewish vegetarian groups and activities in the United States, Britain (where the Jewish Vegetarian Society has its headquarters), and Israel will be discussed. Also, biographies of famous Jewish vegetarians such as Shlomo Goren, the Ashkenazi chief rabbi of Israel, Rabbi

Abraham Kook, Isaac Bashevis Singer, and Yiddish writer I. L.
Peretz will be presented. Finally, an annotated bibliography with
many relevant sources will be included for those who wish more
information on such issues as vegetarianism, nutrition, recipes,
and ideas relating Judaism and vegetarianism.

Judaism has much to say about solutions to the critical problems that face the world today. This book is an attempt to show
how vegetarianism is consistent with Jewish ideals and can play
a role in reducing global problems such as hunger, pollution,
resource depletion, poverty, and violence.

This book is only a beginning of the study of an issue that
must be considered in depth by the Jewish community.

Acknowledgments

Many thanks are due to Mr. Jonathan Wolf, whose course, Judaism and Vegetarianism, at Lincoln Square Synagogue provided the impetus for this work. Several sections of this book reflect his ideas and those of his students with whom I have had the pleasure of studying.

A prime source of ideas and inspiration has been *The Jewish Vegetarian,* the magazine of the Jewish Vegetarian Society, edited by Mr. Philip Pick, the honorary president. Without the existence of this group and its quarterly publication, this project would never have started. Mr. Stanley Rubens, the current president of the society, has also been most helpful by raising issues and questions.

In seeking a wide variety of opinions and sources of information, a first draft of this book was written and circulated for comments to people with a wide variety of backgrounds and interests. I express sincere thanks to all who reviewed the first draft and made valuable suggestions, especially the following: Leon Beer, Aviva Cantor, Rabbi Alfred Cohen, Irving Davidson, Rabbi Chaim Feuerman, Emilio Fischman, Rabbi Stanley Fogel, Sidney Gabel, Martin Garfinkel, Rabbi Everett Gendler, Dudley Giehl, Sally Gladstein, Rabbi Yaakov Goldberg, Hyman Goldkrantz, Robert Greenberg, Teddy Gross, Joseph Harris, Rabbi Fischel Hochbaum, Mel Kimmel, Zvi Kornblum, Deborah Korngold, Dr. Fred Krause, Rabbi David Lazar, Rabbi Joseph Lazarus, Celia Lubianker, Yvette Mandel, Rabbi Jay Marcus, Dr. Shoshana Margolin, Arlene McCarthy, Philip Pick, Murray Polner, Prof.

Margery Robinson, Rabbi H. Rose, Stanley Rubens, Rabbi Murray Schaum, and Rabbi Gerry Serotta.

Jeanne Deutsch, Sidney Gabel, Robert Greenberg, Rabbi Joseph Grunblatt, Rabbi Fischel Hochbaum, Roberta Kalechofsky, and Dr. Shoshana Margolin reviewed the present volume and made significant comments, which are sincerely appreciated. Special thanks to Dr. Shoshana Margolin, who is sharing with us some of her well-researched and clinically successful approaches to guiding people into a vegetarian life-style, based on scientific nutrition.

Thanks also to Melvin Kimmel, attorney, president of the New York chapter of the American Natural Hygiene Society and co-founder of the Society for Natural Living for providing valuable suggestions on many parts of the book, especially the chapters on health and recipes.

Deep appreciation is expressed to George Platt who took the cover and author's photographs with good humor, patience, and professionalism.

Although all of these above people have been very helpful, the author takes full responsibility for the final selection of material and interpretations.

I wish to express deep appreciation to my wife, Loretta, and our children, Susan, David, and Deborah, for their patience, understanding, and encouragement as I used free time from other responsibilities to gather and write this material. They made valuable suggestions on many aspects of this book.

Finally, I wish to thank in advance all who will read this volume and send me ideas and suggestions for improvements so that this book can better help lead toward that day when "none shall hurt nor destroy in all My holy mountain."

RABBINIC ENDORSEMENT

Translated from the Hebrew by Atara Perlman

Congratulations to my friend, Prof. Richard Schwartz; may G-d bless him, for he has worked hard and composed a wonderful work which describes the ideal of vegetarianism and peace of the prophets and sages of Israel as an absolute ideal toward which the laws of our codes and kashrut lead. We look at the vegetarian way of life as a special path of separation and as a step forward toward the "Big Day," i.e., the coming of the Messiah, a day where "Nation shall not lift up sword against nation, neither shall they learn war anymore." (Isaiah 2:4) Bloodshed will cease, and a "Sucking child shall play on the hole of the asp and the weaned child shall put his hand on the basilisk's den." (Isaiah 11:8)

During the Messianic era, when "The lion shall eat straw like the ox," (Isaiah 11:7) man will certainly return to his first stage, before the eating of meat was sanctioned and the consumption of fruits and vegetables will be sufficient. Then there will be total, complete peace between man, his fellowmen, and the animal kingdom. "And the calf and the young lion and the fatling together; And a little child shall lead them." (Isaiah 11:6) Israel and the rest of the world will be blessed, as our Rabbis observed, "Peace was the source of blessings which the Almighty gave to Israel."

Great scholars of Israel, namely the late Chief Rabbi, Harav Abraham Isaac HaCohen Kook, and his outstanding disciple Harav David Cohen, both of blessed memory, expounded admirably in their writings how the laws of the Bible and Talmud mesh with the ideal of peace between man, his fellowmen, and the animal kingdom. This is the desired objective for which we pray and hope.

May it be the will of the Almighty that the number of noble souls will increase amongst our midst, who will be able to observe the dictum of our Rabbis, "Sanctify yourself with that which is permitted unto you"; may they abstain from eating the flesh of living animals and may they be satisfied with the blessings which G-d provided the earth; "And the work of righteousness shall be peace." (Isaiah 32:17) May the knowledge be increased and may the words of the prophet Malachi be realized: "Behold, I will send you Elijah the Prophet before the coming of the great and terrible day of the Lord. And he shall turn the heart of the fathers to their children and the children to their fathers." (Malachi 3:24)

Rabbi Shaar Yashuv Cohen
Chief Rabbi and Rosh Bet Din
Haifa

1

A Vegetarian View of the Bible

God wanted people to be vegetarians, at least at the beginning of human history. This is indicated clearly and explicitly in the first dietary law in the first chapter of Genesis:

> And God said: "Behold, I have given you every herb yielding seed which is upon the face of all the earth, and every tree, in which is the fruit of a tree yielding seed—to you it shall be for food." (Gen. 1:29)

The famous Jewish Bible commentator Rashi states the following about this law:

> God did not permit Adam and his wife to kill a creature and to eat its flesh. Only every green herb shall they all eat together.[1]

Ibn Ezra and other biblical commentators[2] as well as the Talmud[3] agree with this assessment. Yet how many millions of people have read this Torah verse and passed by it without considering its meaning?

The great Jewish philosopher Maimonides states that meat is prohibited because living creatures possess a certain spiritual superiority resembling in some ways the souls of rational beings.[4] In addition, Rabbi Abraham Kook, an outstanding Jew-

1

ish spiritual leader in the early twentieth century, comments on this first dietary law:

> It is inconceivable that the Creator who had planned a world of harmony and a perfect way for man to live should, many thousands of years later, find that this plan was wrong.[5]

After stating that people were to have a vegetarian diet, the Torah next indicates that animals were not to prey on one another but were also to have a vegetarian diet:

> And to every beast of the earth, and to every fowl of the air, and to every thing that creepeth upon the earth, wherein there is a living soul, [I have given] every green herb for food.
> (Gen. 1:30)

Immediately after giving these dietary laws, God saw everything that he had made and "behold, it was very good" (Gen. 1:31). Everything in the universe was as God wanted it, with nothing superfluous and nothing lacking, a complete harmony.[6] Evidently the vegetarian diet was consistent with God's initial plan.

Chapter 5 of Genesis tells us of the long lives of people in the generations from Adam to Noah. Adam lived 930 years; Seth (Adam's son) lived 912 years; Enosh (Seth's son) lived 905 years; Kenan (Enosh's son) lived 910 years; and so on, until Methuselah, who lived 969 years, the longest time of life recorded in the Bible. After the flood, people lived for much shorter periods. Abraham, for example, lived only 175 years.

Why was there such a tremendous change in life spans? Before the flood, people were forbidden to eat meat; after the flood it was permitted. A possible explanation, therefore, is that it was the change in diet that caused the change in life spans. This view is held by the Jewish philosopher and Bible commentator Nachmanides and by I. B. Levinsohn, an early Jewish vegetarian writer.[7] Recent evidence linking heavy meat consumption with several diseases reinforces this point of view (see chapter 3). Of course, a shift to a sensible vegetarian diet will not increase life spans to anywhere near those of early people, but recent medical evidence indicates that it would lead to an increase in the average span of life.

By the time of Noah, humanity had degenerated greatly. "And God saw the earth, and behold it was corrupt; for all flesh had corrupted their way upon the earth" (Gen. 6:12). People had sunk so low that they would eat a limb torn from a living animal. As a concession to people's weakness,[8] permission to eat meat was then given:

> Every moving thing that lives shall be food for you; as the green herb have I given you all. (Gen. 9:3)

Biblical commentator Joseph Albo states that God's commandments were designed to inculcate in people a higher level of spirituality; but in dealing with people as they were, not as they should be, God permitted the eating of meat.[9] Evidently people's appetite for flesh was such that God felt it better to permit the eating of flesh and regulate it rather than to have people harbor a forbidden appetite, which could lead to corruption. Rabbi Kook believes that the permission to eat meat was only a temporary concession and cannot believe that a God who is merciful to his creatures would institute an everlasting law permitting the killing of animals for food.[10]

Just prior to granting Noah and his family permission to eat meat, God stated:

> And the fear of you and the dread of you shall be upon every beast of the earth, and upon every fowl of the air, and upon all wherewith the ground teemeth, and upon all the fishes of the sea: into your hand are they delivered. (Gen. 9:2)

Now that there is permission to eat animals, no longer do people and animals work together in harmony, but every living creature fears and dreads human beings. Rabbi Samson Raphael Hirsch, a famous nineteenth-century Bible commentator, states that the attachment between people and animals was broken and a definite change in the relationship of people to the world began.[11]

The permission given to Noah to eat meat was not uncon-
ditional. There was an immediate prohibition against eating
blood:

> "Only flesh with the life thereof, which is the blood thereof,
> shall ye not eat." (Gen. 9:4)

Similar statements are made in Leviticus 19:26, 17:10,12 and
Deuteronomy 12:16,23,25, and 15:23. The Torah identifies blood
with life: ". . . for the blood is the life" (Deut. 12:23). Life must
already have departed from the animal before it can be eaten.
Rabbi Samuel Dresner states:

> The removal of blood which kashrut teaches is one of the
> most powerful means of making us constantly aware of the
> concession and compromise which the whole act of eating
> meat, in reality, is. Again it teaches us reverence for life.[12]

Immediately after permission was given to eat meat, God stated,
"And surely, your blood of your lives will I require" (Gen. 9:5).
The rabbis base the prohibition of suicide on these words.[13] But
coming directly after flesh is allowed, a vegetarian might specu-
late: Perhaps God is saying that eating meat is a slow form of
suicide. Perhaps God is warning us: "I prefer that you do not
eat meat. But, if you must eat meat, there will be a penalty—
your life blood will I require."[14] That is, your life will be short-
ened by eating something that you were not meant to eat and
that your bodies are not structured to eat (see chapter 3). In
other words, if people choose to live in violence, by slaughtering
and eating animals, they must pay the necessary penalty. Note
that this speculation is consistent with the decrease in life spans
that occurred after permission to eat meat was given and also
with modern research in health and nutrition.

After the Israelites left Egypt, God tried to establish another
nonmeat diet, manna.[15] Manna is described in the Bible as a
vegetarian food, "like coriander seed" (Num. 11:7). The rabbis
of the Talmud stated that the manna had whatever taste and
flavor the eater desired in his heart at the time of eating. It must

also have had sufficient nutrient value because Moses states that "It is the bread which the Lord hath given you to eat (Exod. 16:15).

Rabbi J. H. Hertz comments as follows on the manna: "God in His ever-sustaining providence fed Israel's host during the weary years of wandering in His own unsearchable way."[16]

The manna taught the Children of Israel several lessons, which are interesting from a vegetarian point of view.

(1) God provides for our needs; manna was available for every day's requirements.

In the same way, a vegetarian diet would result in enough food for all. A meat diet leads to scarcity of food for some and the potential for violence (see chapters 4 and 6).

(2) We should be content.[17] Each person was to gather one omer (a measure of manna), but some gathered more and some less. When they measured it out, they found that whether they had gathered much or little, they had just enough to meet their needs.

Again, a vegetarian diet would provide enough for everyone's needs. With a meat-centered diet, the few eat more than they need, and many millions are malnourished.

(3) Enough was provided on Friday morning so that there was no need to gather manna on the Sabbath. The people were commanded to rest on the seventh day.

With a vegetarian diet, people will not need to struggle continually for their means of subsistence. They will be able truly to rest, to have a peaceful Sabbath, knowing that their needs will be taken care of and that there is no reason for violence to obtain necessities.

The people were not satisfied, however, with the simple diet of manna, which sustained them in the desert. The mixed multi-

tude that was with the Jewish people lusted for meat, and the
Children of Israel also wept, saying, "Would that we were given
flesh to eat." They said that they remembered the fish and other
good food that they had in Egypt, but now they had only manna
to eat. The Lord was very angry and Moses was displeased.
Finally, God provided meat in the form of quails, which were
brought by a wind from the sea. While the flesh was in their
mouths, before it was chewed, the anger of God was kindled
against the people; He struck them with a great plague (Num.
11:4-33).

Note the following key points from a vegetarian point of
view: (1) God wanted the people to be sustained on manna; He
was greatly angry when they cried for flesh to eat. (2) God did
provide meat, but a plague broke out among the people. Perhaps
this incident was designed to teach people that they were not
meant to eat meat, and if they did, it would have great negative
consequences. (3) The place where this incident occurred was
named "The Graves of Lust," to indicate that the lust for flesh
led to the many deaths (Num. 11:34).

When the Temple was established, animals could only be
slaughtered and eaten as part of the Temple sacrifice. The great
twelfth-century philosopher and Bible commentator Maimonides
states that the sacrifices were a concession to the primitive practices of the nations at that time.[18] This will be discussed in more
detail in chapter 7, Question 5.

Finally God permitted meat to be eaten even if it wasn't part
of the Temple sacrificial offering:

> When the Lord thy God shall enlarge thy border as He hath
> promised thee, and thou shalt say: "I will eat flesh," because
> thy soul desireth to eat flesh; thou mayest eat flesh, after all
> the desire of thy soul. (Deut. 12:20)

This permitted meat was called *basar ta'avah,* "meat of lust,"
so named because meat is not considered a necessity for life.[19]

The Talmud comments on the preceding Torah statement in
several places:

> The Torah teaches a lesson in moral conduct, that man shall not eat meat unless he has a special craving for it, and shall eat it only occasionally and sparingly.[20]

> Only one who studies Torah may eat meat, but one who does not study Torah is forbidden to eat meat.[21]

Based on this prohibition, how many Jews today can consider themselves so scholarly as to be able to eat meat? And those who do diligently study the Torah and are aware of conditions related to the production and consumption of meat today would, I believe, come to conclusions similar to those in this book.

Rabbi Kook believes that the permission to eat meat "after all the desire of your soul" concealed a shrewd reproach and a qualified injunction.[22] He states that a day will come when people will detest the eating of the flesh of animals because of a moral loathing, and then it shall be said that "because your soul does not long to eat meat, you will not eat meat."[23]

The books of the Bible emphasize vegetarian foods. Flesh foods are often mentioned with distaste and are associated with lust. Israel is described as the land of milk and honey. In the Song of Songs of King Solomon, the divine bounty is mentioned in terms of fruits, vegetables, vines, and nuts. It is significant that there is no special *b'racha* (blessing) recited before eating meat or fish, as there is for other foods such as bread, wine, fruits, and vegetables.

Typical of the Torah's emphasis on nonflesh foods is the following:

> For the Lord thy God bringeth thee into a good land, a land of brooks of water, of fountains and depths, springing forth in valleys and hills; a land of wheat and barley, of vines and fig-trees and pomegranates; a land of olive-trees and honey; a land wherein thou shalt eat bread without scarceness, thou shalt not lack anything in it. . . . And thou shalt eat and be satisfied, and bless the Lord thy God for the good land which He hath given thee. (Deut. 8:7-10)

Along with permission to eat meat, many laws and restrictions (the laws of *kashrut*) were given. Rabbi Kook believes that these regulations imply a reprimand; they are an elaborate apparatus designed to keep alive a sense of reverence for life, with the aim of eventually leading people away from their meat-eating habit.[24]

This idea is echoed by Torah commentator Keli Yakar:

> What was the necessity for the entire procedure of ritual slaughter? For the sake of self-discipline. It is far more appropriate for man not to eat meat; only if he has a strong desire for meat does the Torah permit it, and even this only after the trouble and inconvenience necessary to satisfy his desire. Perhaps because of the bother and annoyance of the whole procedure, he will be restrained from such a strong and uncontrollable desire for meat.[25]

Rabbi Kook sees man's craving for meat as a manifestation of evil rather than an inherent need. He states that meat eating was permitted to prevent cannibalism.[26] He and Joseph Albo believe that in the days of the Messiah people will again be vegetarians.[27] They base this on the prophecy of Isaiah:

> *And the wolf shall dwell with the lamb,*
> *And the leopard shall lie down with the kid;*
> *And the calf and the young lion and the fatling together;*
> *And a little child shall lead them*
> *And the cow and the bear shall feed;*
> *Their young ones shall lie down together,*
> *And the lion shall eat straw like the ox. . . .*
> *They shall not hurt nor destroy in all My holy mountain.*
>
> (Isa. 11:6-9)

Rabbi Kook believes that a virtue of such priceless value (the high moral level involved in the vegetarianism of the generations before Noah), which had once been a possession of humanity, cannot be lost forever.[28] In the future ideal state, just as at the initial period, people and animals will not eat flesh.[29] No one shall hurt or destroy another living creature. People's lives will not be supported at the expense of the lives of animals.

This idea is echoed by the prophet Hosea:

> And in that day will I make a covenant for them with the
> beasts of the field and with the fowls of heaven and with
> the creeping things of the ground. And I will break the bow
> and the sword and the battle out of the land and I will make
> them to lie down safely. (Hos. 2:20)

Rabbi Kook believes that Jewish religious ethical vegetarians are
the pioneers of the messianic era; they are leading a life that
will make the coming of the Messiah more likely.[30]

Today most Jews eat meat, but the high ideal of God, the
initial vegetarian dietary law, still stands supreme in the Bible
for Jews and the whole world to see, the ultimate goal toward
which all people should strive.

2

Tsa'ar Ba'alei Chayim—Judaism and Compassion for Animals

Animals are part of God's creation and people have special responsibilities to them. The Jewish tradition clearly indicates that we are forbidden to be cruel to animals and that we are to treat them with compassion. These concepts are summarized in the Hebrew phrase *tsa'ar ba'alei chayim,* which is the mandate not to cause "sorrow to any living creature."

Psalms 104 and 148 show God's close identification with the beasts of the field, creatures of the sea, and birds of the air. Sea animals and birds received the same blessing as people: "Be fruitful and multiply" (Gen. 1:22). Animals were initially given a vegetarian diet, similar to that of people (Gen. 1:29-30). The important Hebrew term *nefesh chaya* (a "living being" or a "living soul") was applied in Genesis (1:21, 1:24) to animals as well as people. Although the Torah clearly indicates that people are to have "dominion over the fish of the sea, and over the fowl of the air, and over every living thing that creepeth upon the earth" (Gen. 1:28), there was to be a basic relatedness, and the rights and privileges of animals were not to be neglected or overlooked. Animals are also God's creatures, possessing sensitivity and feeling pain; hence they must be treated with compassion, justice, and protection.

God even made treaties and covenants with animals just as with humans:

> "As for me," sayeth the Lord, "behold I establish My Covenant with you and with your seed after you, and with every living creature that is with you, the fowl, the cattle, and every beast of the earth with you; of all that go out of the ark, even every beast of the earth." (Gen. 9:9-10)

As indicated in the previous chapter, God promised the beasts of the field, the fowls of Heaven, and the creeping things of the ground that there would be an end of violence so they would be safe (Hos. 2:20). The Sabbath was proclaimed for animals as well as people (Exod. 20:8-10, 23:12; Deut. 5:14).

God considered animals, as well as people, when he admonished Jonah,

> and should I not have pity on Nineveh, that great city, wherein are more than sixscore thousand persons . . . and also much cattle. (Jon. 4:11)

The Psalmists indicated God's concern for animals, for "His tender mercies are over all His creatures" (Ps. 145:9). They pictured God as "satisfying the desire of every living creature" (Ps. 145:16) and "providing food for the beasts and birds" (Ps. 147:9).

Perhaps the Jewish attitude toward animals is best summarized by the statement in Proverbs 12:10, "The righteous person regards the life of his beast." This is the human counterpoint of "The Lord is good to all, and His tender mercies are over all His creatures" (Ps. 145:9). In Judaism, one who does not treat animals with compassion cannot be regarded as a righteous individual.

BIBLICAL LAWS INVOLVING COMPASSION FOR ANIMALS

(1) It is forbidden to cause pain to any animal.

Maimonides[1] states that this is based on the biblical statement of the angel of God to Balaam, "Wherefore hast thou smitten thine

ass?" (Num. 22:32). This verse is used in the Talmud as a prime
source for its assertion that we are to treat animals humanely.[2]
The *Code of Jewish Law* is more explicit and specific.[3]

> It is forbidden, according to the law of the Torah, to inflict
> pain upon any living creature. On the contrary, it is our duty
> to relieve the pain of any creature, even if it is ownerless or
> belongs to a non-Jew.
>
> When horses, drawing a cart, come to a rough road or a
> steep hill, and it is hard for them to draw the cart without
> help, it is our duty to help them, even when they belong to
> a non-Jew, because of the precept not to be cruel to animals,
> lest the owner smite them to force them to draw more than
> their strength permits.
>
> It is forbidden to tie the legs of a beast or of a bird in a
> manner as to cause them pain.

(2) "Thou shalt not muzzle the ox whên he treadeth out
the corn" (Deut. 25:4).

At the time of threshing, when the ox is surrounded by the food
that he enjoys so much, it should not be prevented from satisfying
its appetite. Rabbi Samson Raphael Hirsch states that this prohibition gives the animal that helps you take possession of the
fruits of the earth a right upon these fruits during its service; no
means may be used to prevent it from eating, whether it be by
calling to it or indirectly by instilling fear, or thirst, or unnecessary separation from the fruits.[4] He cites the Talmud[5] as indicating
that one may prevent an animal from eating when the fruits
might harm it.[6] Rashi, citing Talmud Baba Kamma 54 in support, states that this law also applies to other animals, including
birds.[7]

Professor C. H. Cornill contrasts the humanitarianism of this
law with the grape harvest where "one of the richest Italian real
estate owners fastened iron muzzles to the miserable, fever-
stricken workmen, so that it might not occur to these poor
peasants working for starvation wages under the glowing sun of
Southern Italy, to satiate their burning thirst and their gnawing

hunger with a few of the millions of grapes of the owner."[8] Because of this and similar legislation, William Lecky, the distinguished British historian, states that "tenderness to animals is one of the most beautiful features in the Old Testament."[9]

> (3) "Thou shalt not plow with an ox and an ass together" (Deut. 22:10).

Such an act would cause the weaker animal great pain in trying to keep up with the stronger. The stronger would also suffer by being deprived of its usual routine, by having to act contrary to its instinctive nature. The Talmud extends this law to apply to any case where there are two animals involved, one strong and one weak, and to other activities such as driving carts or wagons.[10]

> You may not allow one task to be done together by animals of two species. You may not allow them to carry the smallest thing together, even if it be only a seed. . . . You may not sit in a wagon drawn by animals of differing species.[11]

Rabbi Hirsch concludes that one should not unite animals for any activities that God's laws of creation have not united for activity in the service of the world.[12]

> (4) "A person should not eat or drink before first providing for his animals."[13]

This is based on Deuteronomy (11:15): "And I will give grass in thy fields for thy cattle, and thou shalt eat and be satisfied." God provides food for the cattle before people and we are to imitate Him.

According to R. Eleazer ha-Kapar, a talmudic sage, no one should buy a domestic animal, wild beast, or bird unless he is able to feed it properly.[14] The duty to feed an animal first is so great that a person may interrupt the performance of a rabbinic commandment in order to ascertain that this has been done. For example, a person may, after saying the benediction over bread, not immediately eat the bread in order to inquire as to whether the animals have been fed.[15]

(5) Animals too must be able to rest on the Sabbath day.

> Remember the Sabbath day, to keep it holy. Six days shalt thou labor, and do all thy work; but the seventh day is a sabbath unto the Lord, thy God, in it thou shalt not do any manner of work, thou, nor thy son, nor thy daughter, nor thy man-servant, nor thy maid-servant, nor thy *cattle,* nor thy stranger that is within thy gates. (Exod. 20:8-10)

The *kiddush* (sanctification over wine or grape juice) that is recited on the Sabbath includes this verse.

> Six days thou shalt do thy work, but on the seventh day thou shalt rest; that thine *ox* and thine *ass* may have rest, and the son of thy handmaid, and the stranger, may be refreshed. (Exod. 23:12)

Based on these biblical statements, Rashi states that animals must be free to roam on the Sabbath day and graze freely and enjoy the beauties of nature.[16] The fact that animals are considered within the Ten Commandments indicates the emphasis placed on compassion for animals in Judaism. Rabbi Hertz, in commenting on Exodus 20:10, states:

> It is one of the glories of Judaism that, thousands of years before anyone else, it so fully recognized our duties to the dumb friends and helpers of man.[17]

(6) "It is forbidden to kill a newborn ox, sheep, or goat until it has had at least seven days of warmth and nourishment from its mother" (Lev. 22:27).

This commandment shows the desire of the Torah to spare the feelings of living creatures and to instill a spirit of mercy in people. Then why did God permit the killing of animals at all?

It was a concession to people's weakness and to the primitive practices of many nations during the biblical period.

(7) "And whether it be ox or ewe, ye shall not kill it and its young both in one day" (Lev. 22:28).

This forbids a custom, usual in foreign cults, of sacrificing an animal and its young together. Maimonides comments on this verse as follows:

> It is prohibited to kill an animal with its young on the same day, in order that people should be restrained and prevented from killing the two together in such a manner that the young is slain in the sight of the mother; for the pain of animals under such circumstances is very great. There is no difference in this case between the pain of man and the pain of other living beings, since the love and the tenderness of the mother for her young ones is not produced by reasoning but by feeling, and this faculty exists not only in man but in most living things.[18]

(8) We are forbidden to take the mother bird and its young on the same day.

> If a bird's nest chance to be before thee in the way, in any tree or on the ground, with young ones or eggs, and the dam sitting upon the young, or upon the eggs, thou shalt not take the dam with the young; thou shalt in any wise let the dam go, but the young thou mayeth take unto thyself; that it may be well with thee, and that thou mayest prolong thy days.
> (Deut. 22:6-7)

For the compassion that we show to the mother bird, we are promised a long life. Maimonides comments that when the mother bird is sent away she does not see the taking of her young ones and does not feel any pain at that time.[19] Furthermore, in most cases, the commandment will result in the entire nest being left untouched, because the young or the eggs, which people are allowed to take, are generally unfit for food.[20] He also states that if we are commanded not to cause grief to animals and to birds, how much more careful must we be not to cause grief to people.[21]

(9) Animals should not be allowed to suffer pain.

> If thou see the ass of him that hateth thee lying under its burden, thou shalt surely not pass by him; thou shalt surely release it with him. (Exod. 23:5)

This commandment has both a humane motive toward the animal and a charitable motive toward an enemy. The talmudic rabbis taught that the greatest hero is a person who turns an enemy into a friend.[22] The Talmud states that the obligation to relieve an animal from pain or danger superceded rabbinic ordinances related to the Sabbath.[23]

(10) The rabbis strongly disapproved of hunting as a sport.[24]

A Jew was permitted to capture fish, flesh, or fowl only for purposes of human food or some other practical human need. Based on the statement "not to stand in the way of sinners" (Ps. 1:1), the Talmud prohibited association with hunters.[25] A query was addressed to Rabbi Ezekiel Landau (1713-93) by a man wishing to know if he could hunt in his large estate, which included forests and fields. The response stated:

> In the Torah the sport of hunting in imputed only to fierce characters like Nimrod and Esau, never to any of the patriarchs and their descendants. . . . I cannot comprehend how a Jew could even dream of killing animals merely for the pleasure of hunting. . . . When the act of killing is prompted by that of sport, it is downright cruelty.[26]

(11) Although the Torah contains no general rule prohibiting cruelty to animals, there are so many commands mandating humane treatment for them that the rabbis explicitly declared that consideration for animals is biblical law.[27] Hence, various rabbinic Sabbath laws

could be relaxed to show compassion to or avoid harm to an animal. For such purposes, one has permission to capture them,[28] take care of their wounds when they are fresh and painful,[29] race them to exhaustion as a remedy for overeating,[30] place them in water to cool them following an attack of congestion,[31] and raise them from water into which they have fallen.[32]

(12) *Shechitah* (Jewish ritual slaughter).

Because, as indicated previously, the consumption of meat was permitted as a concession to people's weakness, it was desired to make slaughter as painless as possible through *shechitah* (the laws of ritual slaughter). The laws of *shechitah* provide the most humane way of slaughtering animals.[33] The knife to be used is regularly examined to ensure that it is perfectly smooth, without a notch that might tear the flesh. The arteries to the head of the animal are severed by the cut, thus stopping blood circulation to the head and making the animal oblivious to any pain. The slaughterer, the *shochet,* must be carefully chosen. He is obligated to examine the animal for any possible disease and to slaughter the animal according to Jewish law. The *shochet* is required to be a pious and learned person. He must prove his complete knowledge of the laws of *shechitah.* He must recite a blessing prior to slaughter as a reminder that he must have reverence for the life that he takes. Thus the laws of *shechitah* teach that meat-eating is a concession to people's weakness. Question 6 in chapter 7 will consider *shechitah* further.

(13) On Yom Kippur, the most sacred day of the Jewish year, when all Jews fast and pray for life and good health from God in the coming year, it is forbidden to wear leather shoes. The reason is related to our behavior toward God's creatures; it is not proper to plead for compassion when one has not shown compassion toward other living creatures.[34]

Rabbi Moses Isserles, known as the Ramah, states: "How can a man put on shoes, a piece of clothing for which it is necessary to kill a living thing, on Yom Kippur, which is a day of grace and compassion, when it is written 'His tender mercies are over all His works' (Ps. 145:9)."[35]

Although Jews are required to recite a special benediction, "Blessed are thou, O Lord our God, King of the Universe, who has kept us in life, and hast preserved us, and has enabled us to reach this season," when putting on a piece of clothing for the first time, an exception is made for furs and leather shoes because an animal had to be killed in making them.[36]

The *Code of Jewish Law*[37] has a similar statement:

> It is customary to say to one who puts on a new garment: "Mayest thou wear it out and acquire a new one." But we do not express this wish to one who puts on new shoes or a new garment made of fur or leather . . . because a garment like this requires the killing of a living creature, and it is written: "And His mercy is upon all his works (Ps. 145:9).

EXAMPLES OF KINDNESS TO ANIMALS SHOWN BY GREAT JEWISH HEROES

The truly great Jewish heroes of the Bible were trained for their tasks by being shepherds of flocks.

Moses was tested by God through his shepherding. When Moses was tending the sheep of Jethro in the wilderness of Midian, a young kid ran off from the flock. Moses ran after it until he found the kid drinking by a pool of water. Moses approached it and said, "I did not know that you ran away because you were thirsty; now, you must be tired." So Moses placed the kid on his shoulders and carried him back to the flock. Then God said, "Because thou has shown mercy in leading the flock, thou will surely tend My flock, Israel."[38]

God also deemed David worthy of tending the Jewish people because he knew how to look after sheep, bestowing upon each the care it needed. David used to prevent the larger sheep from going out before the smaller ones. The smaller ones were then able to graze upon the tender grass. Next he permitted the old sheep to feed from the ordinary grass, and finally the young, lusty sheep at the tougher grass.[39]

Rebecca was judged suitable as Isaac's wife because of the kindness she showed to animals. Eleazar, Abraham's servant, asked Rebecca for water for himself. She not only gave him water but also ran to provide water for his camels. Rebecca's concern for camels was evidence of a tender heart and compassion for all God's creatures. It convinced Eleazar that Rebecca would make a suitable wife for Isaac (Gen. 24:11-20).

The patriarch Jacob also demonstrated concern for animals. After their reconciliation, his brother Esau said to him, "Let us take our journey and let us go, and I will go before thee." But Jacob, concerned about his flocks and children, politely replied: "My lord knoweth that the children are tender, and that the flocks and the herds giving suck are a care to me; and if they overdrive them one day, all the flocks will die. Let my lord, I pray thee, pass over before his servant and I will journey on gently, according to the pace of the cattle that are before me and according to the pace of the children, until I come unto my lord, unto Seir" (Gen. 33:12-14).

STORIES RELATED TO COMPASSION TO ANIMALS FROM THE JEWISH TRADITION

> Rabbi Judah, the Prince, was sitting and studying the Torah in front of the Babylonian Synagogue in Sepphoris, when a calf passed by as if pleading, "Save me!" Rabbi Judah said to it, "What can I do for you? For this you were created." As a punishment for his heartlessness, he suffered from a toothache for thirteen years.

> One day, a creeping thing (a weasel) ran past his daughter who was about to kill it. He said to her, "My daughter, let it be, for it is written, 'and his tender mercies are over all his works' (Ps. 145:9)." Because Rabbi Judah prevented an act of cruelty and unkindness to an animal, his health was restored to him.[40]

Significant in this regard is the response of Ga'on R. Sherina in his *Opinions* to the following inquiry:[41] "If Rabbi Judah was punished because he handed a calf over to the slaughterer, and was once again rewarded because he protected a dumb creature from death, should we learn from this not to slaughter any animal and not to kill harmful animals?" The Ga'on's answer: "Animals that may harm people, such as snakes, lions, wolves, must always be killed; on the other hand, animals that do us no harm and are not needed for food or medicine should not be killed. . . . To save a calf that we *need* for nourishment is not required of us."[42]

Now that we know that we do *not* need meat for nourishment, and as a matter of fact, the consumption of flesh products harms our health, what a tremendously powerful argument for vegetarianism is in this story and the commentary.

Rabbi Israel Salanter, one of the most distinguished Orthodox Rabbis of the nineteenth century, failed to appear one Yom Kippur eve to chant the sacred Kol Nidre Prayer. His congregation became concerned, for it was inconceivable that their saintly rabbi would be late or absent on this very holy day. They sent out a search party to look for him. After much time, their rabbi was found in the barn of a Christian neighbor. On his way to the synagogue, Rabbi Salanter had come upon one of his neighbor's calves, lost and tangled in the brush. Seeing that the animal was in distress, he freed it and led it home through many fields and over many hills. His act of mercy represented the rabbi's prayers on that Yom Kippur evening.[43]

Rabbi Zusya once was on a journey to collect money to ransom prisoners. He came to an inn and in one room found a large cage with many types of birds. He saw that the birds wanted to fly out of the cage and be free again. He burned with pity for them and said to himself, "Here you are, Zusya, walking your feet off to ransom prisoners. But what greater ransoming of prisoners can there be than to free these birds from their prison?" He then opened the cage, and the birds flew out into freedom.

When the innkeeper saw the empty cage, he was very angry and asked the people in the house who had released the birds. They answered that there was a man loitering around who appeared to be a fool and that he must have done it. The innkeeper shouted at Zusya: "You fool! How could you rob me of my birds and make worthless the good money I paid for them?" Zusya replied: "You have often read these words in the Psalms: 'His tender mercies are over all His work'?" Then the innkeeper beat Zusya until he became tired and then he threw him out of the house. And Zusya went his way serenely.[44]

Rabbi Abramtzi was a man full of compassion—his compassion was for all living things—He would not walk on the grass of the field lest he trample it down. He was very careful not to tread on grasshoppers or crawling insects. If a dog came to the door of his house—he would instruct the members of his household to feed the animal. In winter he would scatter crumbs of bread and seed on the window sills. When sparrows and other birds arrived and began to pick at the food, he could not remove his gaze from them and his face would light up with joy like that of a little child—He looked after his horses far better than his coachmen did. When travelling and the coach had to ascend an incline, he would climb down in order to lighten the load and more often than not he would push the cart from behind. On summer days he would compel his coachman to stop on the way and turn aside to a field in order that the horses should rest and partake of the pure green grass. The rabbi loved these rest periods in the forest. While the horses were grazing—he would sit under a tree and interest himself in a book. At times he would pray in the field or the forest. This gave him great pleasure, for he used to say, "The field and the forest are the most beautiful and finest of the Houses of the Lord."

It happened once that the rabbi was on the road on a Friday. It would take another three hours to reach home.

Due to the rain the road was in a mess. The wagon could only proceed with difficulty—The mud gripped the wheels and slowed down its progress. It was mid-day and they had not even completed half the journey. The horses were tired and worn out. They had no energy to proceed further.

The *tzaddik* (saint) told the driver to stop and to give fodder to the horses, so that they could regain their strength. This was done. Afterwards the journey was continued, but the going was heavy and the wagon sunk up to the hubs of the wheels in the mud. In fact it was with the greatest difficulty that the horses maintained their balance in the swampy ground. The vapour of sweat enveloped their skin. Their knees trembled and at any moment they would have to rest. The coachman scolded and urged them on. He then raised his whip on the unfortunate creatures. The *tzaddik* grabbed him by the elbow and cried out: "This is cruelty to animals, cruelty to animals." The coachman answered in fury: "What do you want me to do? Do you want us to celebrate the Sabbath here?"

"What of it?" replied the rabbi quietly. "It is better that we celebrate the Sabbath here than cause the death of these animals by suffering. Are they not the creatures of the Lord? See how exhausted they are. They have not the energy to take one more step forward."

"But what of the Sabbath? How can Jews observe the Sabbath in the forest?" asked the coachman.

"My friend, it does not matter. The Sabbath Queen will come to us also here, for her glory fills the whole world, and particularly in those places where Jews yearn for her. The Lord shall do what is good in His eyes. He will look after us, supply us with our wants and guard us against all evil.[45]

TREATMENT OF ANIMALS TODAY

As we have seen, the Jewish tradition stresses compassion for animals and commands that we strive to avoid causing them pain (*tsa'ar ba'alei chayim*). Unfortunately, the conditions under which animals are raised for food today are quite different from any the Torah would endorse.

Chickens are raised for slaughter in long, windowless, crowded sheds, where they never see sunlight, breathe fresh air, or get any exercise.[46] From hoppers suspended from the roof, they obtain food and water, along with many chemical additives according to a programmed schedule. Crowding is so bad that chickens can't even stretch both wings at one time. The results of these very unnatural conditions are potential feather-pecking and cannibalism. To avoid this, the lighting is kept very dim, the chickens are given special contact lens, and more drastically, they are "de-beaked." De-beaking involves cutting off part of the chicken's beak while its head is held in a guillotine-like device, a very painful process.

Ruth Harrison describes the results of her observations of current methods of raising chickens in her excellent book, *Animal Machines*. She found that the chickens seemed to have lost their minds; their eyes gleamed through the bars, they viciously pecked at any hand within reach, and they pulled feathers out of other chickens' backs looking for flesh and blood to eat.[47]

There is tremendous cruelty in the forced feeding of ducks and geese to produce paté de foie gras.[48] Foie gras literally means fat liver. It is the liver of a goose or duck, monstrously fattened by having 60 to 80 pounds of corn inserted by force down its gullet. The farmer generally holds the neck of the goose between his legs, pouring the corn with one hand and massaging it down the neck with the other. When this process is no longer effective, a wooden plunger is used to compact it still further. The bird suffers unimaginable pain, and as the liver grows to a monstrous size, sclerosis of the liver develops. Finally, after 25 days of such agony, when the bird is completely stupefied with pain and unable to move, it is killed and the gigantic liver, considered a delicacy, is removed. Currently machines are used to force feed birds to make the process more "efficient," with greater resultant agony.

Although it would seem impossible to top the cruelties described in the previous cases, perhaps this occurs in raising veal calves. After being allowed to nurse for only 2 or 3 days, the veal calf is removed from its mother, with no consideration of its need for motherly nourishment, affection, and physical contact. The calf is locked in a small slotted stall with not enough space to move around, stretch, or even lie down. To obtain the pale, tender veal desired by consumers, the calf is purposely kept anemic by giving it a special high-calorie, iron-free diet. The calf craves iron so much that it would lick the iron fittings on its stall and its own urine if permitted to do so; it is prevented by having its head tethered to the stall so that it cannot even turn around. The stall is kept very warm and the calf is not given any water, so that it will drink more of its high-caloric liquid diet. The very unnatural conditions of the veal calf, its lack of exercise, sunlight, and fresh air, its lack of proper food and water, its lack of any emotional stimulation make for a very sick, anemic animal. Antibiotics and drugs are used to keep the calf from other illnesses and death. The calf leaves its pen only when ready for slaughter; sometimes it drops dead from the exertion of going to slaughter.

The transportation of animals by rail or truck involves additional cruelties.[49] They are jammed into a confined area for many hours, sometimes days, where they suffer from lack of food, water, exercise, and ventilation. They are often exposed to extreme heat, cold, and humidity. They are generally not fed for the last 24 to 48 hours prior to slaughter.

The horrible treatment of animals raised for food is summarized in the following two selections:

> How far have we the right to take our domination of the animal world? Have we the right to rob them of all pleasures in life simply to make more money more quickly out of their carcasses? Have we the right to treat living creatures solely as food converting machines? At what point do we acknowledge cruelty?[50]

> Every year millions of animals are born and bred for the sole purpose of satisfying those who like the taste of meat. Their lives vary in length from a few weeks to a few years; most live a fraction of the time they would in more natural conditions. They die in slaughter-houses where, if the tranquilizers have their effect, they know only a few moments of the awful fear of death before they are stunned, and their throats cut. This is what all meat-eaters actively support, for there would be no batteries, no sweat-boxes, no need to castrate male animals or artificially inseminate females, no cattle markets and no slaughter-houses if there was no one insensitive enough to buy their products. It is simply impossible to farm animals for food without imprisoning, mutilating and eventually slaughtering them, and no one can ignore this price that has to be paid for the pleasure of eating meat.[51]

As the previous examples indicate, the conditions under which animals are raised today are completely contrary to the Jewish ideals of compassion and avoiding *tsa'ar ba'alei chayim*. Instead of animals being free to graze on the Sabbath day and enjoy the beauties of creation, they are confined for all of their lives to darkened, crowded cells without air, natural light, or the ability to exercise. Whereas the Torah mandates that animals should be able to eat the products of the harvest as they thresh in the fields, today animals are given chemical fatteners and other additives in their food, based on computer programs. Where Judaism indicates consideration for animals by mandating that a strong and weak animal not be yoked together, veal calves spend their entire lives standing on slats, their necks chained to the sides, without sunlight, fresh air, or exercise. Jews who continue to eat meat are helping to support a system contrary to basic Jewish principles and commandments.

3

Preserving Health and Life

Judaism regards the preservation of physical well-being as a religious command of great importance. Jews are to take care of their health and do nothing that may unnecessarily endanger themselves. Life is regarded as the highest good and we are obliged to protect it.

An important Jewish principle is *pikuach nefesh,* the duty to save a human life. The talmudic sages applied the principle "Ye shall therefore keep my statutes and ordinances, which if a man do he shall live by them" (Lev. 18:5) to all the laws of the Torah. Hence Jews are to be more particular about matters concerning danger to health and life than about ritual matters.[1] If it could help save a life, one *must* (not may) violate the Sabbath, eat forbidden foods, and even eat on Yom Kippur.[2] The only laws that could not be violated to preserve a life were those prohibiting murder, idolatry, and sexual immorality.[3]

According to the Torah, we are not allowed to place ourselves intentionally in danger; it states "take heed to thyself and take care of your lives" (Deut. 4:9) and, again, "take good care of your lives (Deut. 4:15).

The Bible, Talmud, and *Codes of Jewish Law* stress the avoidance of danger through the positive commandment of making a parapet (wall) for one's roof so that no one will fall from the roof (Deut. 22:8). Rabbi Hertz, in his commentary on this commandment, states that failure to protect human life

26

exposes one to guilt for the spilling of blood, in God's eyes.[4] The talmudic sages extended this prohibition to cover all cases where negligence endangers life, such as placing a broken ladder against a wall or keeping a dangerous dog.[5]

In his classic Mishneh Torah, Maimonides indicates a variety of prohibitions, all based on the necessity to do everything possible to preserve life:

> It makes no difference whether it be one's roof or anything else that is dangerous and might possibly be a stumbling block to someone and cause his death—for example, if one has a well or a pit, with or without water, in his yard—the owner is obliged to build an enclosing wall ten handbreadths high, or else to put a cover over it lest someone fall into it and be killed. Similarly, regarding any obstacle which is dangerous to life, there is a positive commandment to remove it and to beware of it, and to be particularly careful in this matter, for Scripture says, *Take heed unto thyself and take care of thy life* (Deut. 4:9). If one does not remove dangerous obstacles and allows them to remain, he disregards a positive commandment and transgresses the prohibition: *Thou bring not blood* (Deut. 22:8).
>
> Many things are forbidden by the Sages because they are dangerous to life. If one disregards any of these and says, "If I want to put myself in danger, what concern is it to others?" or "I am not particular about such things," disciplinary flogging is inflicted upon him.
>
> The following are the acts prohibited: One may not put his mouth to a flowing pipe of water and drink from it, or drink at night from rivers or ponds, lest he swallow a leech while unable to see. Nor may one drink water that has been left uncovered, lest he drink from it after a snake or other poisonous reptile has drunk from it, and die.[6]

Maimonides's statements clearly indicate that Judaism absolutely prohibits the placing of one's health or life into possible danger. He disallows the popular rationalization, "What concern is it to others if I endanger myself?"

There are similar prohibitions against endangering one's life in Karo's *Shulchan Aruch* and other *Codes of Jewish Law*.[7] In

Choshen Mishpat 427, Karo devotes an entire chapter to "the
positive commandment of removing any object or obstacle which
constitutes a danger to life." In his glossary on Karo's *Shulchan
Aruch,* Rabbi Moses Isserles (the Ramah) concludes:

> One should avoid all things that might lead to danger because
> a danger to life is stricter than a prohibition. One should be
> more concerned about a possible danger to life than a possible
> prohibition. Therefore, the Sages prohibited one to walk in a
> place of danger such as near a leaning wall (for fear of
> collapse), or alone at night (for fear of robbers). They also
> prohibited drinking water from rivers at night . . . because
> these things may lead to danger . . . and he who is concerned
> with his health [lit.: watches his soul] avoids them. And it is
> prohibited to rely on a miracle or to put one's life in danger
> by any of the aforementioned or the like.[8]

The Talmud tells that Rabbi Huna, the greatest Torah authority of his generation, would personally inspect all the walls of his
town of Sura before the onset of the winter storms. Any he found
unsafe, he would order torn down. If the owner could not afford
to rebuild the wall, Rabbi Huna would pay for it from his own
funds.[9]

Suicide, whether rapid or slow, is absolutely prohibited in
Jewish law. This is, as indicated earlier, based on the biblical
phrase, "and surely your blood, the blood of your lives, will I
require" (Gen. 9:5). As will be discussed later in this section,
there is evidence showing that eating meat constitutes a slow
form of suicide.

Rabbinic literature is specific in its stress on proper hygiene
to protect health. The human body is considered as a sanctuary.[10]
The importance of good and regular meals is stressed[11] and the
rabbis give much advice on foods conducive to health.[12] They
stress the importance of personal cleanliness and washing daily
in honor of God.[13] The talmudic sage Hillel considered it a
religious commandment to bathe in order to protect his health.[14]

As will be discussed in detail in chapter 5, the Jewish sages
prohibit the unnecessary destruction of anything of value. The
extension of this prohibition to include the willful destruction

of one's own body is made by Rabbi Israel Lipshuetz, known as *Tifereth Yisroel.*[15]

Rabbi Samson Raphael Hirsch, writing in *Horeb,* where he analyzes the commandments, speaks very powerfully of the mandate to preserve health and life:

> Limiting our presumption against our own body, God's word calls to us: "Do not commit suicide!" "Do not injure yourself!" "Do not ruin yourself!" "Do not weaken yourself!" "Preserve yourself!"[16]

> You may not in any way weaken your health or shorten your life. Only if the body is healthy is it an efficient instrument for the spirit's activity. . . . Therefore, even the smallest unnecessary deprivation of strength is accountable to God. Every smallest weakening is partial murder. Therefore you should avoid everything which might possibly injure your health. . . . And the law asks you to be even more circumspect in avoiding danger to life and the limb than in the avoidance of other transgressions.[17]

People use a number of arguments to justify the continuance of a dangerous habit, such as smoking, or to mitigate against the imposition of a rabbinic ban on such habits, based on Jewish law. But in every case, these arguments can be rejected in the face of *pikuach nefesh,* the requirement to preserve life.[18]

It would seem from the preceding discussions that if it can be clearly and convincingly shown that the consumption of meat is dangerous to people's health, it should be prohibited by Jewish law.

RESULTS WHEN PEOPLE HAVE LIVED UNDER VEGETARIAN DIETS

During World War I, Denmark was cut off from its meat supply because of a blockade by the Allied forces. To avoid acute food shortages, the government sought the aid of Denmark's vegetarian society. Dr. Mikkel Hindhede wrote about the results in the *Journal of the American Medical Association.* He pointed out that only the wealthy could afford to buy meat, and most of the population ate bran, bread, barley, porridge, potatoes, greens, milk, and some butter.[19] This nearly vegetarian diet led to better health and reduced mortality rates (17%) for the Danish people during the first year of the new diet.[20]

A similar thing happened in Norway when food rationing was instituted during World War II and the consumption of meat was sharply cut. Because of the reduction in animal fats consumed, the Norwegian death rate dropped from 31 per 10,000 people in 1938 to about 20 per 10,000 people in 1944.[21] After the war, when the prewar diets resumed, the mortality rate rose sharply, reaching 26 per 10,000 people in 1946.[22]

Unlike the short wartime experiences of the Danes and Norwegians, many Seventh-Day Adventists have followed a vegetarian diet for over 100 years. They also abstain from smoking, alcohol, coffee, tea, spices, hot condiments, and highly refined products. A recent study of their health shows that colonic, rectal, and intestinal cancer are 50-70% lower than in the general population.[23]

In another study of Seventh-Day Adventist women, about half of whom were vegetarian, lower blood pressure and a rate of endometrial cancer 40% lower than women in the general population were found.[24]

An Australian study found the blood pressures of Seventh-Day Adventist vegetarians, 30-79 years old, to be "significantly less" than the levels found in nonvegetarian controls.[25] The study concludes that dietary factors, probably intake of animal protein, animal fat, or another dietary component associated with them, are likely to be responsible for the differences in blood-pressure readings.[26]

After studying the mainly vegetarian diet of the Hunzas of Kashmir, noted for their longevity, Major-General Sir Robert McCarrison, once physician to the king of England, states: "I never saw a case of asthenic dyspepsia, of gastric or duodenal ulcer, of appendicitis, or mucus colitis or cancer."[27]

Dr. Paul Dudley White, the famous heart specialist, visited the Hunzas in 1964. His studies show that the 90- and 110-year-old men tested showed no evidence of heart disease. He stated that there is a correlation between their diet and lifestyles and the low incidence of heart disease.[28]

The Bible contains an interesting case of people eating only vegetarian foods. The Book of Daniel tells how Daniel and his three companions were captives in the court of Nebuchadnezzar, king of Babylon. They refused to defile themselves with the king's meat and wine, which were not kosher. The king's servant was fearful that their health would suffer and the king would blame him. But Daniel said: "For ten days, give us pulse (peas, beans, and lentils) to eat and water to drink. Then let our countenances be looked upon before thee, and the countenance of those children that eat of the portion of the king's meat; and as thou seeth, deal with thy servants." The king's servant consented to wait the period and "at the end of the ten days their countenances appeared fairer and fatter in flesh than all the children who did eat the portion of the king's meat." The king's servant then took away from the others their meat and wine and fed them also pulse and water (Dan. 1:8-16).

ILLNESSES RELATED TO MEAT CONSUMPTION

(a) HEART DISEASE

Medical authorities are finding increasing evidence linking arteriosclerosis, a thickening of the walls of arteries associated with heart attacks and strokes, to meat-centered diets, which are high in saturated fats and cholesterol. The American Heart Association has stated:

> Studies have indicated that many people who show no evidence of heart disease are increasing their risk of heart attack by following a diet that is high in saturated fat and cholesterol. The typical American diet . . . tends to raise the level of cholesterol in the blood, and a high blood cholesterol contributes to the development of arteriosclerosis.[29]

The *Journal of the American Medical Association* states: "A vegetarian diet can prevent 90 percent of our thrombo-embolic disease and 97 percent of our coronary occlusions."[30]

Statistics indicate that populations of countries where meat consumption is high (U. S., Canada, Australia) have high mortality rates from heart disease. Populations of developed countries with the lowest meat consumption (Italy and Japan) have considerably lower mortality rates from heart disease.[31]

The negative effects of meat consumption start early. A study of American men, ages 19-22, killed in the Korean War shows a high degree of arteriosclerosis, compared with similar-aged Koreans, who were relatively free of this disease.[32] Although the Koreans were basically vegetarians, the American diet consisted largely of milk, butter, eggs, and meat.

In 1970, an Inter-Society Commission for Heart Disease Resources, composed of 29 voluntary health agencies including the American Medical Association, investigated what the American public should do to stem the "epidemic" of arteriosclerosis and heart attacks. A key recommendation was that there should be less meat in the diet so that there would be reductions of dietary cholesterol, dietary saturated fat, and total fat. They also recommended that the diet contain more fruits, vegetables, grains, and legumes.[33]

In 1977, an important document, *Dietary Goals for the United States,* was adopted and published by a Senate Select Committee on Nutrition and Human Needs. They also recommended that the American diet have less cholesterol, saturated fat, and total fat, that the consumption of red meat be reduced, and that there be added consumption of whole grains, fruits, and vegetables.[34]

The last two studies cited indicate that top scientific and political groups are stressing the need for improved diets, with less red meat and increased consumption of vegetarian foods.

Based on a variety of scientific studies, Dr. John A. Scharffenberg, an associate professor of applied nutrition and a director of a community health education program concludes:

It is now known that serum cholesterol and thus arteriosclerosis can be reduced by proper diet. Morbidity and mortality rates from coronary heart disease also can be lowered by dietary means.[35]

He suggests, consistent with the previously discussed studies, that people adopt a "prudent diet," one low in fat, meat, and cholesterol and high in fruits, whole grains, vegetables, and legumes.

Nutritionist Nathan Pritikin, founder of the Longevity Centre and Longevity Research Institute in California, feels that Jews can reduce heart disease, hypertension, and other diseases by switching to a low-fat, low-protein, high-carbohydrate diet. He claims that "the average Jewish diet must have been designed by the enemies of the Jewish people."[36]

(b) CANCER

There have been several recent studies in the United States and other countries aimed at investigating whether there is a connection between meat eating and various forms of cancer. In 1975, at the Symposia on Nutrition in the Causation of Cancer, Dr. Ernest L. Wydner stated that dietary factors could be related to as much as 50% of all cancers found in women and a third of all cancers found in men.[37]

Breast Cancer. There is evidence that shows a positive correlation between a diet heavy in animal fats and the incidence of breast cancer.[38] Most breast cancers are found in the populations of countries where people eat large amounts of animal fat, such as the United States, Great Britain, Australia, Argentina, and Canada. In countries where little animal fat, particularly beef, is consumed, breast cancer rates are extremely low. European Jewish women living in Israel are three times more likely to get breast cancer than Asian or Oriental Jews. Japanese women in the United States are four times more likely to develop breast cancer than their counterparts in Japan.[39]

Cancer of the Colon. Dr. Frey Ellis, a consultant hematologist at Kingston Hospital, Surrey, England, states:

Cancer of the colon is about twenty times more common in meat eaters than in people who eat a lot of vegetables. This suggests that transit time through the bowel is involved. Meat takes three or four days to go through the intestine, whereas vegan foods, which are high in fiber content, take only twenty-four hours.[40]

Dr. Ernest L. Wydner, president of the American Health Foundation, recently stated: "We believe that a diet high in animal protein and animal fat correlates with a high incidence of colon cancer."[41]

(c) KIDNEY DISEASE

The consumption of meat creates more waste products, hence more strain on the kidneys. Commenting on this, Dr. John H. Kellogg states:

Comparative analyses of the urine of low protein feeders and those who take an ordinary mixed diet show that even moderate meat eaters require of their kidneys three times the amount of work in elimination of nitrogenous wastes that is demanded of the kidneys of flesh abstainers. While the kidneys are young, they are usually able to bear this extra burden so that no evidence of injury appears; but as they become worn with advancing age they become unable to do their work efficiently.[42]

People who suffer from chronic kidney disorders are often treated with a dialysis machine, which aids the kidneys in removing waste products from the blood. Such people can significantly increase the time between treatments through a flesh-free diet.[43]

(d) FOOD POISONING

Over one million cases of food poisoning are reported every year in the United States. Salmonella organisms are responsible in most instances. Meat and poultry products are the usual vehicles of contamination. Vegetarians are rarely bothered by these seldom fatal, but often incapacitating, illnesses.[44]

REASONS WHY EATING MEAT IS HARMFUL

(a) PEOPLE ARE NOT "DESIGNED" TO EAT MEAT

Scientists generally agree that human beings are not naturally suited for a diet that includes flesh. The French naturalist Baron Cuvier states: "Fruits, roots, and the succulent parts of vegetables appear to be the natural food of man."[45] Geoffrey Hodson quotes the great Swedish naturalist Linnaeus as follows: "Man's structure, external and internal, compared with that of other animals, shows that fruit and succulent vegetables constitute his natural food."[46] The following comparisons support these statements:[47]

(1) Our small and large intestines, like those of other primates, measure four times our height; for carnivores, they are the same as their body length. Because of the long intestines, meat passes very slowly through the human digestive system; it takes about 5 days during which the disease-causing products of decaying meat are in constant contact with the digestive organs (vegetarian food takes only about 1½ days).[48]

(2) Our hands are similar to those of apes; they are meant for picking food such as vegetables, fruits, leaves, flowers, seeds, etc., and not for tearing flesh.

(3) Our lower jaw, or mandible, can move both up and down and side to side, like the primates'; carnivores' jaws move only up and down.

(4) Our saliva is alkaline like that of the higher species of apes; it contains ptyalin to digest carbohydrates. Carnivores' saliva is acidic.

(5) Unlike carnivores, we do not have fangs for biting into flesh. Our so-called canine teeth are not truly canine

like the dog's. We are not constituted to prey upon
animals, rip apart their bodies, or bite into their flesh.
We are designed for gentler activities in obtaining our
food.

(6) Although our gastric secretions are acidic like that of
carnivores, their stomachs have four times as much acid;
this strong acidic region is necessary to digest their
high-protein flesh diet.

(7) Carnivores have proportionally larger kidneys and livers
than we have; they need these larger organs in order to
handle the excessive nitrogenous waste of a flesh diet.

(8) The carnivores' livers secrete a far greater amount of
bile into the gut to deal with their high-fat meat diet.

Table I indicates that people are closest in structure to animals
that primarily eat fruits.

That our natural instinct is not toward flesh food is stated by
R. H. Wheldon:

> The gorge of a cat, for instance, will rise at the smell of a
> mouse or a piece of raw flesh, but not at the aroma of fruit.
> If a man can take delight in pouncing upon a bird, tear its
> still living body apart with his teeth, sucking the warm blood,
> one might infer that Nature had provided him with carniv-
> erous instinct, but the very thought of doing such a thing
> makes him shudder. On the other hand, a bunch of luscious
> grapes makes his mouth water, and even in the absence of
> hunger, he will eat fruit to gratify taste.[49]

(b) CONDITIONS UNDER WHICH ANIMALS ARE RAISED TODAY

The terrible conditions under which animals are raised today
lead to unhealthy animals, which result in poor health for people.
In the foreword to Ruth Harrison's book *Animal Machines,*
Rachel Carson states:

> As a biologist whose special interest lies in the field of
> ecology, or the relation between living things and their en-

TABLE I

Structural Comparison of Humans to Animals

Meat eater	Leaf-grass eater	Fruit eater	Human beings
Has claws	No claws	No claws	No claws
No pores on skin; perspires through tongue to cool body	Perspires through millions of pores on skin	Perspires through millions of pores on skin	Perspires through millions of pores on skin
Sharp, pointed front teeth to tear flesh	No sharp, pointed front teeth	No sharp, pointed front teeth	No sharp, pointed front teeth
Small salivary glands in the mouth (not needed to predigest grains and fruits)	Well-developed salivary glands, needed to predigest grains and fruits	Well-developed salivary glands, needed to predigest grains and fruits	Well-developed salivary glands, needed to predigest grains and fruits
Acid saliva; no enzyme ptyalin to predigest grains	Alkaline saliva; much ptyalin to predigest grains	Alkaline saliva; much ptyalin to predigest grains	Alkaline saliva; much ptyalin to predigest grains
No flat, back molar teeth to grind food	Flat, back molar teeth to grind food	Flat, back molar teeth to grind food	Flat, back molar teeth to grind food
Much strong hydrochloric acid in stomach to digest tough animal muscle, bone, etc.	Stomach acid 20 times less strong than meat eaters	Stomach acid 20 times less strong than meat eaters	Stomach acid 20 times less strong than meat eaters
Intestinal tract only 3 times body length so rapidly decaying meat can pass out of body quickly	Intestinal tract 10 times body length; leaf and grains do not decay as quickly and can pass more slowly through the body	Intestinal tract 12 times body length; fruits do not decay as rapidly and can pass more slowly through the body	Intestinal tract 12 times body length

SOURCE: Barbara Parkham *What's Wrong with Eating Meat?* Denver Colo.: Amanda Marga Publications, 1979, p. 23. Reproduced with permission.

vironment, I find it inconceivable that healthy animals can be produced under the artificial and damaging conditions that prevail in the modern factory-like installations, where animals are grown and turned out like so many inanimate objects. The crowding of broiler chickens, the revolting insanitary conditions in the piggeries, the lifelong confinement of laying hens in tiny cages. . . . This artificial environment is not a healthy one. Diseases sweep through these establishments, which indeed are kept going only by the continuous administrations of antibiotics. Disease organisms then become resistant to the antibiotics. . . . The menace to human consumers from the drugs, hormones, and pesticides used to keep this whole fantastic operation somehow going is a matter never fully explored.[50]

Exercise is a must for animals in their natural state. When animals are denied exercise (as generally occurs today with modern factory methods), their complete metabolism is influenced. Their meat becomes infested with waste (metabolism poison), which would have disappeared if the animals had been permitted to exercise.[51]

Other factors that negatively affect human health are hormones, tranquilizers, antibiotics, which are administered to animals, radioactive substances, which they ingest with their food, and sodium nitrate, sodium nitrite, and sodium sulfite, which are used as antispoilage agents in many prepared meats. These agents have all been shown to be cancer causing.[52]

Just before and during slaughter, the terrified animal's biochemistry changes profoundly. The entire carcass is pain-poisoned by toxic by-products that are forced throughout the body. Large amounts of hormones, especially adrenalin, remain in the meat and later enter and poison human tissue. The Nutrition Institute of America has stated, "The flesh of an animal carcass is loaded with toxic blood and other waste by-products."[53]

(c) NEGATIVE EFFECTS OF PESTICIDES

Pesticides and other pollutants increase to serious proportions as we move up the food chain. The following is the build up of a pollutant in a food chain, starting with one unit of pollution in water:[54]

```
        1—water            ⎫
       10—phytoplankton    ⎬  microscopic organisms
      100—zooplankton      ⎭
    1,000—shrimps
   10,000—small fish
  100,000—medium fish
1,000,000—large fish
10,000,000—chicken living on fish meal
```

At each ascending level of the food chain, the effect of the pollutant is magnified about ten times. One unit of pollution in water can be increased by a factor of millions by the end· of a food chain. Hence the concentration of environmental poisons is many times larger in meat and fish than in vegetarian foods.

This huge magnification of pollutants as one goes higher up on the food chain has led to some concern about dangerous chemicals being transmitted from nursing mothers to their infants. Numerous studies have shown that breast feeding has many positive benefits for both mothers and babies. It is the best food for the baby, as it has all the necessary nutrients, decreases the chances for allergies, and represents the only completely adequate food for the first 6 months.[55]

However, recently, an Environmental Protection Agency study of 1,400 women in 46 states found widespread contamination with such dangerous substances as DDT, dieldrin, and PCB in mothers' milk. The Environmental Defense Fund has published a booklet called "Birthright Denied: The Risks and Benefits of Breast Feeding,"[56] in which it indicates that in many cases the amount of these chemicals in breast milk is well above levels regarded as safe. The group advises women who are contemplating nursing their babies to have their breast milk tested.

Vegetarian women have been found to have one-third to one-half the levels of pesticides of women having nonvegetarian diets. A young woman considering nursing her child should strongly consider these findings. Because breast feeding has so many benefits, a shift toward a vegetarian diet could be a major step toward healthier babies, as well as healthier mothers.

In an interview, Stephanie Harris of the Environmental Defense Fund states:

> If you're a heavy meat consumer we recommend you nurse once a day and supplement with bottle feeding. But if your diet is—and has been—very low in animal fats, one can assume that the residues in your body will be lower; the benefits of breast feeding will then outweigh the risks. . . . If you're planning on becoming pregnant and especially if you plan on nursing, then become a vegetarian or reduce your consumption of animal fats by other dietary methods.[57]

For more information on breast feeding, you may write to La Leche League, 9619 Minneapolis Avenue, Franklin Park, Illinois 60131, or to the Environmental Defense Fund, 1525 18 Street, N.W., Washington, D. C. 20036.

Medical and statistical evidence demonstrates that the eating of flesh is hazardous to health and can lead to fatal diseases. Thus, the numerous halachic rules prohibiting dangerous activities should be extended to include the eating of flesh. Such an extension by leading rabbinic authorities of our time, preferably acting jointly and with proper publicity, would save many lives and improve the health and life expectancy of the Jewish people.

4

Feeding the Hungry

On Yom Kippur, while fasting and praying for a good year, Jews are told through the words of the Prophet Isaiah that fasting and prayers are not sufficient; they must work to end oppression and share with the hungry:

> Is not this the fast that I have chosen? To loose the chains of wickedness, to undo the bonds of oppression, and to let the oppressed go free. . . . Is it not to share thy bread with the hungry? (Isa. 58:6-7)

The importance of feeding the hungry is a fundamental principle in Judaism. The Talmud states, "Aiding the poor and hungry weigh as heavily as all the other commandments of the Torah combined."[1] The *Midrash* teaches:

> God says to Israel, "My children, whenever you give sustenance to the poor, I impute it to you as though you gave sustenance to Me. . . ." Does then God eat and drink? No, but whenever you give food to the poor, God accounts it to you as if you gave food to Him.[2]

On Passover we are reminded not to forget the poor and needy. Besides providing *ma'ot chittim* (charity for purchasing matzah) for the poor before Passover, at the seders, we say:

Lo! This is the bread of affliction which our
ancestors ate in the land of Egypt.
Let all who are hungry come and eat.
Let all who are in need come and celebrate the Passover.[3]

We are even admonished to feed our enemies, if they are in need:

If your enemy is hungry, give him bread to eat.
If your enemy is thirsty, give him water to drink. (Prov. 25:21)

Today, about half of the world's people are not receiving an adequate amount of food.[4] Between 10 and 20 million people die annually of hunger and its effects.[5] In some areas, 20-40% of the children do not reach the age of 5.[6] Many who survive suffer permanent mental or physical retardation or have diseases that curb their ability to function effectively. It is feared that with population rising rapidly, especially in the poorer countries, more people will receive inadequate diets in the future.

One important reason that many are starving today is the tremendous amount of grains used to fatten animals for slaughter. Meat-centered diets are very wasteful of grain, land, water, fuel, and fertilizer.

Not only is much land and many resources used in the United States to raise beef, but the United States is also the world's largest importer of beef.[7] We import approximately 1 million head of cattle every year from Mexico, half as much beef as all Mexicans have left for themselves.[8] In spite of widespread poverty and malnutrition in Honduras, they export large amounts of beef to the United States. Beef for export in Honduras is grown by a tiny wealthy elite (0.3% of the total population) who own over 25% of all cultivable land.[9]

Georg Borgstrom, author of *The Hungry Planet,* points out that protein-starved underdeveloped countries actually export more protein to wealthy nations than they receive. He calls this "the protein swindle." Ninety percent of the world's fish meal catch, for example, is exported to rich countries. Borgstrom states:

Sometimes one wonders how many Americans and western
Europeans have grasped the fact that quite a few of their

beef steaks, quarts of milk, dozens of eggs, and hundreds of broilers are the result, not of their agriculture, but of the approximately two million metric tons of protein, mostly of high quality, which astute Western businessmen channel away from the needy and hungry.[10]

It is a fundamental Jewish belief that God provides enough for all. In our daily prayers, it is said, "He openeth up his hand and provideth sustenance to all living things" (Ps. 145:16). Jews are obligated to give thanks to God for providing enough food for us and for all of humanity. In the *bircat hamazon* (grace after meals), the following opening prayer is recited:

Blessed art thou, O Lord our God, King of the universe, who feedest the whole world with goodness, with grace, with loving kindness and tender mercy; thou givest food to all flesh, for thy loving kindness endureth forever. Through thy great goodness, food hath never failed us: Oh may it not fail us for ever and ever for thy great name's sake, since thou nourishest and sustainest all beings, and doest good unto all, and providest food for all thy creatures whom thou hast created. Blessed art thou, O Lord, who givest food unto all.[11]

The blessing is correct. God *has* provided enough for all. The bounties of nature, properly distributed and properly consumed, would sustain all people. Millions of people are hungry today, not because of insufficient agricultural capacity, but because of unjust social systems and wasteful methods, including the feeding of tremendous amounts of grains to animals.

Judaism teaches involvement and concern with the plight of fellow human beings. Every life is sacred and we are obliged to do what we can to help others. The Torah states, "Thou shalt not stand idly by the blood of thy brother" (Lev. 19:16).

We speak out justifiably against the silence of the world when 6 million Jews and 5 million others were murdered in the Holocaust. Can we be silent when millions die agonizing deaths because of lack of food? Can we acquiesce to the apathy of the world to the fate of starving people?

As Elie Wiesel and others have pointed out, we should not

lightly invoke analogies with the Holocaust. Writing in *Sh'ma,*
David M. Szonyi makes connections between the current global
hunger crisis and the Holocaust:

> On the news recently, I learned of a U.S. Dept. of Agri-
> culture report predicting that 10 million children will die of
> malnutrition in the coming year. As a Jew living after the
> Holocaust, I cannot help but think of "10 million" as 4
> million more than 6 million. And when thinking of the 6
> million, I tend to feel more anger at the silent complicity of
> the living than to think of the bitter grief of the dying. For
> it is the world of the indifferent that surrounds me every-
> where, that I have inherited and find myself a part of.
>
> One generation later, we the living manage to muddle by
> well enough, to live our lives with only occasional grumbles
> about "soaring inflation." We contrive to live our lives by
> shutting our eyes to those who can't live theirs, anonymous,
> purportedly "perpetually," hungry masses who suffer mal-
> nutrition not so much from international food shortages
> as from international indifference. And yet, the Talmud tells
> us that if one saves a single human life, it is as if one saved
> a whole world. What then if one allows a single life to wither
> and perish? Or a thousand or 10 million?[12]

Even during the Holocaust, people had rationalizations to
justify their apathy. Jewish history should sensitize us to the evil
of silence.

The Hebrew prophets berated those who were content and
comfortable while others were in great distress:

> *Tremble you women who are at ease,*
> *Shudder you complacent ones;*
> *Strip and make yourselves bare,*
> *Gird sackcloth upon your loins.* (Isa. 32:11)

> *Woe to those who are at ease in Zion. . . .*
> *Woe to those who lie upon beds of ivory*
> *And stretch themselves upon their couches. . . .*
> *Who drink wine from bowls*
> *And anoint themselves with the finest oils*
> *But are not grieved at the ruin of Joseph.* (Amos 6:1-7)

Rabbi Marc H. Tannenbaum, National Interreligious Affairs Director of the American Jewish Committee, in his testimony before the Ad Hoc Senate Committee Hearings on World Hunger spelled out why Jews must be involved in helping the hungry today:

> If one takes seriously the moral, spiritual, and humanitarian values of Biblical, Prophetic, and Rabbinic Judaism, the inescapable issue of conscience that must be faced is: How can anyone justify not becoming involved in trying to help save the lives of starving millions of human beings throughout the world—whose plight constitutes the most agonizing moral and humanitarian problem in the latter half of the 20th century?[13]

We must be involved. We must speak out. We must act. Some of the ways Judaism teaches us to be involved in helping the hungry are to pursue justice, practice charity, show compassion, and share our resources with others.

The pursuit of justice, of a just society, is one of the most fundamental concepts of Judaism. Note two things about the following important statement in Deuteronomy (16:20): "Justice, justice shalt thou pursue." First, the word "justice" is repeated. This is a very infrequent occurrence in the Torah. When words are repeated, it is generally to add emphasis. Second, we are told to *pursue* justice. Hence we are not to wait for the right opportunity, the right time and place, but are to pursue or run after opportunities to practice justice.

The psalmists wrote: "Give justice to the weak and the fatherless; maintain the right of the afflicted and the destitute" (Ps. 82:3-4).

The prophet Amos cries out that God does not only want sacrifices, but

> *Let justice well up as waters,*
> *and righteousness as a mighty stream.* (Amos 5:24)

Isaiah tells us

The Lord of Hosts shall be exalted in justice,
The Holy God shows Himself holy in righteousness.

Isa. 5:16)

Proverbs stresses that

To do righteousness and justice is preferred by
God above sacrifice (Prov. 21:3)

Rabbi Emanuel Rackman points out that Judaism teaches a special kind of justice, an "emphatic justice," which

> . . . seeks to make people identify themselves with each other —with each other's needs, with each other's hopes and aspirations, with each other's defeats and frustrations. Because Jews have known the distress of slaves and the loneliness of strangers, we are to project ourselves into their souls and make their plight our own.[14]

He points out that in 36 places in the Torah we are commanded not to mistreat the stranger in our midst.[15]

Many times in Jewish history, we have known hunger and famine. Because of famines, Abraham was forced to go to Egypt (Gen. 12:10), Isaac went to the land of Avimelech, king of the Philistines, in Gerar (Gen. 26:1), the Children of Israel went to Egypt to buy grain (Gen. 42:1-3), and Naomi and her family fled Israel and went to Moab (Ruth 1:1-2). There were also famines in the reigns of King David (2 Sam. 21:1) and King Ahab (1 Kings 18: 1-2).

Jews know the travail of great hunger. The Prophet Jeremiah states: Happier were the victims of the sword than the victims of hunger, who pined away, stricken by want of the yield of the field (Lam. 4:9).

Based on Jewish values and Jewish history, we must identify with the starving masses of the world. One way to practice emphatic justice is through vegetarian diets, which do not utilize disproportionate amounts of the earth's resources.

To help the poor and hungry, Judaism places great stress on

the giving of charity. The Hebrew word for charity (*tzedakah*) literally means righteousness. In the Jewish tradition, *tzedakah* is not an act of condescension from one person to another who is in need. It is the fulfillment of a *mitzvah,* a commandment, to a fellow human being, who has equal status before God.

Maimonides rules that:

> He who refuses to give or gives less than he should according to his means, the court can compel him to give his share and can apply corporal punishment. Members of the court can enter his property and confiscate the amount they feel he should give. They can do this even on the eve of the Sabbath.[16]

In the Jewish tradition, failure to give charity is equivalent to idolatry. So important was the giving of charity by Jews that Maimonides was able to say: "Never have I seen or heard of a Jewish community that did not have a charity fund."[17]

Maimonides defines the various types of charity and categorizes them into his famous "eight degrees of charity"; the highest form is to help a person to become self-supporting, through a gift, a loan of money, or teaching the person a trade.[18]

Judaism places emphasis on charity because of the great difficulties that poor people face:

> If all afflictions in the world were assembled on one side of the scale and poverty on the other, poverty would outweigh them all.[19]

Judaism believes that poverty is destructive to the human personality and negatively shapes a person's life experiences. "The ruin of the poor is their poverty" (Prov. 10:15). "Where there is no sustenance, there is no learning."[20] "The world is darkened for him who has to look to others for sustenance."[21] "The sufferings of poverty cause a person to disregard his own sense (of right) and that of his maker."[22]

The negative effects of poverty are so severe that the Talmud makes the startling statement that "the poor person is considered as if he were dead."[23] Judaism does not encourage an ascetic life. Insufficiency of basic necessities does not ease the path toward holiness.

Many Jewish concepts are designed to aid the poor: the corners of the field are to be left uncut for the poor to pick (Lev. 19:9); the gleanings of the wheat harvest and fallen fruit are to be left for the poor (Lev. 19:10); during the sabbatical year, the land is to be left fallow so that the poor (as well as animals) may eat of whatever grows freely (Lev. 25:2-7).

Failure to treat the poor properly is a desecration of God: "Whoso mocketh the poor blasphemeth his maker" (Prov. 17:5). Our father Abraham always went out of his way to aid the poor. He set up inns on the highways so that the poor and the wayfarer would have access to food and drink when in need.[24]

Closely related to the Jewish values of justice and charity is the importance the Jewish tradition places on compassion. The entire Torah is designed to teach us to be compassionate: "The purpose of the laws of the Torah is to promote compassion, loving-kindness and peace in the world."[25] The Talmud teaches that "Jews are compassionate children of compassionate parents, and one who shows no pity for fellow creatures is assuredly not of the seed of Abraham, our father."[26] The rabbis considered Jews to be distinguished by three characteristics: compassion, modesty, and benevolence.[27] As indicated previously, we are to feel empathy for strangers, "for we were strangers in the land of Egypt" (Deut. 10:19). The *bircat hamazon* (grace recited after meals) speaks of God feeding the whole world with compassion.

While in Egypt, Joseph had two sons during the seven good years of food production, but no children during the seven years of famine. The great Jewish commentator Rashi interprets this to mean that while people are starving, others who have enough should engage in acts of self-denial to show compassion and sympathy.[28]

We are not only to have compassion for Jews, but for all who are in need.

> Have we not all one Father? Hath not one God created us?
> Why, then, do we deal treacherously with one another,
> Profaning the covenant of our ancestors? (Mal. 2:10)

> Are you not like the Ethiopians to Me, O people of Israel?
> says the Lord. Did I not bring up Israel from the land of
> Egypt and the Philistines from Caphtor and the Syrians from
> Kir? (Amos 9:7)

As indicated previously, we are to help even our enemies when
they lack sufficient food or water (Prov. 25:21).

Rabbi Hirsch writes very eloquently of the importance of
compassion:

> Do not suppress this compassion, this sympathy, especially
> with the sufferings of your fellowman. It is the warning voice
> of duty, which points out to you your brother in every
> sufferer, and your own sufferings in his, and awakens the
> love which tells you that you belong to him and his sufferings
> with all the powers that you have. Do not suppress it! . . .
> See in it the admonition of God that you are to have no joy
> so long as a brother suffers by your side.[29]

But just having compassion for the poor and hungry is not
enough. A fundamental Jewish principle is that those who have
much should share with others who are less fortunate. Rabbi
Hillel stresses that we must not only be concerned with our own
welfare. "If I am not for myself, who will be for me? But if I
am for myself alone, what am I?"[30] Also, as previously indicated,
the *Haggadah,* which we read at the Passover seder, exhorts us
to share. We are to reach out to all who are hungry and in need.
The act of prolonging one's meal, on the chance that a poor
person may come so that one may give him food is so meritorious
that the table of the person who does this is compared to the altar
of the ancient Temple.[31]

Judaism's great emphasis on sharing is also illustrated in the
following chasidic tale:

> The story is told of a great rabbi who is given the privilege
> of seeing the realms of Heaven and Hell before his death.

He was taken first to Hell where he was confronted with a huge banquet room in the middle of which was a large elegant table covered with a magnificent white table cloth, the finest china, silver and crystal. The table was covered from one end to the other with the most delicious foods that the eyes have ever seen or the mouth tasted. And all around the table people were sitting looking at the food . . . and wailing. It was such a wail that the rabbi had never heard such a sad sound in his entire life and he asked, "With a luxurious table and the most delicious food, why do these people wail so bitterly?" As he entered the room he saw the reason for their distress. For although each was confronted with this incredible sight before him, no one was able to eat the food. Each person's arms were splinted so that the elbows could not bend. They could touch the food but could not eat it. The anguish this caused was the reason for the great wail and despair that the rabbi saw and heard.

He was next shown Heaven, and to his surprise he was confronted by the identical scene witnessed in Hell. (The large banquet room, the elegant table, the lavish settings and the sumptuous foods. And in addition, once again everyone's arms were splinted so the elbows could not bend.) Here, however, there was no wailing, but rather joy greater than he had ever experienced in his life. For whereas here too the people could not put the food into their own mouths, each picked up the food and fed it to another. They were thus able to enjoy not only the beautiful scene, the wonderful smells, and the delicious foods, but the joy of sharing and helping one another.[32]

Rabbi Jay Marcus of Young Israel of Staten Island commented on the fact that *karpas* (eating of greens) and *yahatz* (breaking of the middle matzah for later use as the dessert) are next to each other in the Passover seder service:[33] Only those who can live on simple things like greens (vegetables, etc.) will be able to divide their possessions and share with others.

Vegetarianism is consistent with this Jewish concept of sharing. As Jay Dinshah, former president of the North American Vegetarian Society, states:

After all, vegetarianism is, more than anything else, the very essence and the very expression of altruistic SHARING, . . .

> the sharing of the One Life, . . . the sharing of the natural resources of the Earth, . . . the sharing of love, kindness, compassion, and beauty in this life.[34]

While millions starve, it is imperative that those who have much simplify their lives so they can share more with others.

A group of outstanding religious leaders, including representatives of different branches of Judaism in the United States and Israel met in Bellagio, Italy, in May 1975 to consider "The Energy/Food Crisis: A Challenge to Peace, a Call to Faith." They agreed on a statement that included this assertion:

> The deepest and strongest expression of any religion is the "styles of life" that characterizes its believers. It is urgent that religious communities and individuals scrutinize their life style and turn from habits of waste, overconsumption, and thoughtless acceptance of the standards propogated by advertisements and social pressures.
>
> The cry from millions for food brought us together from many faiths. God—Reality itself—calls us to respond to the cry for food. And we hear it as a cry not only for aid but also for justice.[35]

Simpler life styles, with less wasteful diets, can be an important first step toward justice for the hungry of the world. Simpler diets do not imply a lack of joy or a lack of fellowship. As Proverbs 15:17 states: "Better a dinner of herbs where love is than a stalled ox with hatred."

During the Middle Ages, local Jewish councils sometimes set up "sumptuary laws" for the community; people were forbidden to spend more than a limited amount of money at weddings and other occasions. These laws were designed so that the poor should not be embarrassed at not being able to match the expenditures of the wealthy and so that a financial strain was not placed on the community as a whole. Perhaps the spirit of such laws should be invoked today. Can we continue to consume flesh that wastes so much grain at a time when many are starving? Is it not now time for officiating rabbis to specify guidelines to reduce waste and ostentation at weddings, bar mitzvahs, and other occasions?

Can a shift to vegetarian diets make a difference with regard to world hunger? Consider these statistics:

(1) Two hundred and twenty million Americans are eating enough food (largely because of the high consumption of grain-fed livestock) to feed over 1 billion people in the poor countries.[36]

(2) The world's cattle consume an amount of food equivalent to the calorie requirements of 8.7 billion people.[37]

(3) If the average American were to reduce consumption of meat and poultry by 10%, over 12 million tons of grain would become available for food.[38]

These facts indicate that the food being fed to animals in the affluent nations could, if properly distributed, end both hunger and malnutrition throughout the world. A switch from flesh-centered diets would free land and other resources, which could be used to grow nutritious crops for people. It would then be necessary to promote policies that would enable people in the underdeveloped countries to use their resources and skills to become food self-reliant.

With so much hunger, poverty, and injustice in the world, explicit Jewish mandates to feed the hungry, help the poor, share resources, practice charity, show compassion, and pursue justice and the trials and tribulations of Jewish history point to vegetarianism as the diet most consistent with Jewish values.

5

Judaism, Vegetarianism, and Ecology

A fundamental Jewish principle is that "the earth is the Lord's and the fullness thereof" (Ps. 24:1). Many principles in the Torah are related to this concept.

(1) People are to be co-workers with God in helping to preserve and improve the world.

There is a *Midrash* (a story that teaches a Torah lesson based on biblical events and values) that beautifully expresses the idea that God needs people to help tend the world:

> *In the hour when the Holy one, blessed be He,*
>   *created the first man,*
> *He took him and let him pass before all the trees of*
>   *the Garden of Eden and said to him:*
> *"See my works, how fine and excellent they are!*
> *Now all that I have created, for you have I created.*
> *Think upon this and do not corrupt and desolate My World,*
> *For if you corrupt it, there is no one to set it*
>   *right after you."*[1]

The talmudic sages had great concern about preserving the environment and preventing pollution. They stated: "It is for-

bidden to live in a town which has no garden or greenery."[2]
Threshing floors had to be placed far enough from a town so that
it would not be dirtied by chaff carried by winds.[3] Tanneries had
to be kept at least 50 cubits from a town and could be placed
only on the east side of a town, so that odors would not be carried
by the prevailing winds from the west.[4] The rabbis felt a sense
of sanctity toward the environment when they said "the climate
of the land of Israel makes one wise."[5]

    (2) Everything belongs to God. We are to be stewards of
        the earth, to see that its produce is available for all
        God's children.

There is an apparent contradiction between two verses in
Psalms: "The earth is the Lord's" (Ps. 24:1) and "The heavens
are the heavens of God, but the earth He has given to the children
of man" (Ps. 115:16). The apparent discrepancy is cleared up
in the following way: Before a person says a *b'racha* (a blessing),
before he acknowledges God's ownership of the land and its
products, then "the earth is the Lord's"; after a person has said a
b'racha, acknowledging God's ownership and that we are merely
stewards to see that God's works are properly used and shared,
then "the earth He has given to the children of man."[6]
Property is a sacred trust given by God; it must be used to
fulfill God's purposes. No person has absolute or exclusive control over his or her possessions. The concept that people have
custodial care of the earth, as opposed to ownership is illustrated
by this story from the Talmud:

> Two men were fighting over a piece of land. Each claimed
> ownership and bolstered his claim with apparent proof. To
> resolve their differences, they agreed to put the case before
> the rabbi. The rabbi listened but could come to no decision
> because both seemed to be right. Finally he said, "Since I
> cannot decide to whom this land belongs, let us ask the land."
> He put his ear to the ground and, after a moment, straightened
> up. "Gentlemen, the land says it belongs to neither of you—
> but that you belong to it."[7]

As indicated previously, even the produce of the field does not belong solely to the person who farms the land. The poor are entitled to a portion:

> And when ye reap the harvest of your land, thou shalt not wholly reap the corner of thy field, neither shalt thou gather the gleaning of thy harvest. And thou shalt not glean thy vineyard, neither shalt thou gather the fallen fruit of thy vineyard; thou shalt leave them for the poor and for the stranger; I am the Lord, thy God. (Lev. 19:9-10)

These portions set aside for the poor were not voluntary contributions based on kindness. They were, in essence, a regular divine assessment. Because God was the real owner of the land, he claimed a share of his own gifts for the poor.

As a reminder that "the earth is the Lord's," the land must be permitted to rest and lie fallow every seven years (the sabbatical year):

> And six years thou shalt sow thy land, and gather in the increase thereof, but the seventh year thou shalt let it rest and lay fallow, that the poor of thy people may eat; and what they leave, the beast of the field shall eat. In like manner thou shalt deal with the vineyard, and with thy oliveyard.
> (Exod. 23:10-11)

One of the reasons for the sabbatical year is ecological. The land was given a chance to rest and renew its fertility.

(3) We are not to waste or destroy unnecessarily anything of value.

This prohibition, called *bal tashchit* ("thou shalt not destroy") is based on the following Torah statement:

> When thou shalt besiege a city a long time, in making war against it to take it, thou shalt not destroy (*bal tashchit*) the trees thereof by wielding an ax against them; for thou mayest eat of them but thou shalt not cut them down; for is the tree

of the field man, that it should be besieged of thee? Only the
trees of which thou knoweth that they are not trees for food,
them thou mayest destroy and cut down, that thou mayest
build bulwarks against the city that maketh war with thee,
until it fall. (Deut. 20:19-20)

This prohibition against destroying fruit-bearing trees in time
of warfare was extended by the Jewish sages. It is forbidden to
cut down even a barren tree or to waste anything if no useful
purpose is accomplished.[8] The sages of the Talmud made a general prohibition against waste: "Whoever breaks vessels or tears
garments, or destroys a building, or clogs up a fountain, or
destroys food violates the prohibition of *bal tashchit*."[9] In summary, *bal tashchit* prohibits the destruction, complete or incom-
plete, direct or indirect, of all objects of potential benefit to
people.

The seriousness with which the rabbis considered the violation of *bal tashchit* is illustrated by the following talmudic statements: "The great scholar Rabbi Hanina attributed the early
death of his son to the fact that the latter had chopped down a
fig tree."[10] "Jews should be taught when very young that it is a
sin to waste even a little food."[11] All that God has created was
meant for human welfare and sustenance. Therefore, to waste
and destroy is to sin against God as well as against one's fellow
human beings.

Rabbi Samson Raphael Hirsch states that *bal tashchit* as the
first and most general call of God: We are to "regard things as
God's property and use them with a sense of responsibility for
wise human purposes. Destroy nothing! Waste nothing!"[12] He
further states that "destruction . . . also means trying to attain a
certain aim by making use of more things and more valuable
things when fewer and less valuable ones would suffice."[13]

The following talmudic teaching related to *bal tashchit* has
special applicability to vegetarianism:

> Two men entered a shop. One ate coarse bread and vegetables,
> while the other ate fine bread, fat meat, and drank old wine.
> The one who ate fine food suffered harm, while the one who

had coarse food escaped harm. Observe how simply animals live and how healthy they are as a result.[14]

Unfortunately, the wisdom of *bal tashchit* is seldom applied today. Our society is based on waste, on buying, using, and throwing away. Advertisements constantly try to make us feel guilty if we do not have the newest gadgets and the latest styles of clothing. Every national holiday has become an orgy of consumption.

Our flesh-centered diets are extremely wasteful:

(1) The average person in the United States eats almost five times as much grain (mostly in the form of animal products) as does a person in an undeveloped country.[15]

(2) It takes about 8 lb. of grain to produce 1 lb. of beef in a feedlot;[16] in terms of protein, the ratio is approximately 20 lb. of grain protein to 1 lb. of beef protein.[17]

(3) Over 80% of the grain grown in the United States is fed to animals.[18] Perhaps the modern counterpart of destroying fruit-bearing trees is taking grains which could feed starving people, and feeding them to animals.

(4) Half of our agricultural land is devoted to feed-crops.[19]

(5) A nonvegetarian diet requires about 3.5 acres/person, whereas a total vegetarian (vegan) diet only requires about a fifth of an acre.[20] Hence, a shift to vegetarian diets would free much valuable land, which could be used to grow nutritious crops for people.

(6) The standard diet of a person in the United States requires 2500 gal. of water/day (for animals' drinking water, irrigation of crops, processing, washing, cooking, etc.).[21] A person on a pure vegetarian diet requires as little as 300 gal./day.[22]

(7) A nonvegetarian diet also wastes much energy. In the United States, an average of 10 calories of fuel energy are required for every calorie of food energy obtained; in many other countries, they gain 20 or more calories of food energy per calorie of fuel energy.[23]

As these facts indicate, a vegetarian diet is far less wasteful than a meat-centered diet and is therefore much more consistent with the commandment of *bal tashchit*.

Modern agricultural methods related to meat production are a prime cause of the environmental crises facing the United States and much of the world today.

(1) The tremendous quantity of grains grown to feed animals requires extensive use of chemical fertilizer and pesticides. Much air and water pollution is caused by the production and use of these products. Various constituents of fertilizer, particularly nitrogen, are washed into surface waters. High levels of nitrates in drinking water have caused illnesses for people as well as animals.[24]

(2) Mountains of manure produced by cattle raised in feedlots wash into and pollute streams, rivers, and underground water sources. American livestock produce about 2 billion tons of waste annually—more than ten times that produced by humans.[25]

(3) Large areas of land throughout the world have been destroyed by grazing animals. Overgrazing has been a prime cause of erosion in various parts of the world throughout history.

(4) Slaughterhouses are also prime sources of pollution. One study revealed that 18 meat-packing companies in Omaha, Nebraska, discharge over 100,000 lb. of grease, carcass dressing, carcass cleaning, intestinal waste, paunch manure, and fecal matter from viscera into the sewer system that empties into the Missouri River.[26]

Demand for meat in the wealthy countries also leads to environmental damage in the poor countries. In Brazil, the cutting down of trees to clear land for ranches to raise cattle for export is a major cause of the destruction of tropical rain forests.[27] Eric Eckholm of the World Watch Institute predicts that continued destruction of these forests for a few more decades would change the nature of life on this planet for all time.[28]

Contrary to one purpose of the sabbatical year, the fertility of cleared soil has been greatly reduced in recent years by over-use and heavy utilization of chemical fertilizers and pesticides. Philip Pick, editor of the *Jewish Vegetarian,* points out that only under a vegetarian economy can the sabbatical year be observed today:

> It [the sabbatical year] does not provide for shiploads of fodder to be removed from the land and exported to feed factory farm birds and beasts incarcerated. . . . The wastages would be too great; over ninety percent of this produce is lost in conversion to flesh, and the undernourished people in the grain growing countries would suffer still further by the denial of the Sabbath produce of their land. Indeed the present system of factory farming would not be possible if the Sabbatical were recognized.[29]

It is interesting to note that the sabbatical year provided for beasts of the field to eat from that which would grow freely on farms, vineyards, and oliveyards. What a tremendous difference this is from current practices of chemical feeding of animals in darkened cells where they spend all their wretched lives.

The concept of the sabbatical year is one answer to people's problems today. Consider one year without tremendous amounts of chemicals and fertilizers that pollute our air and water and reduce the fertility of the soil. Consider the benefits to people of getting away for a year from their lives of hustle and bustle, from the shrieking of the marketplace, from the constant need to amass more and more goods; instead there could be a utilization of time toward mental and spiritual development and perhaps a study of methods of reducing economic and military disputes.

Vegetarianism means a simplification of life and far less stress on the environment. Land presently used to grow feed crops could be used to raise food for hungry people and to lay fallow periodically, thus enabling it to improve its productivity. Far less chemical fertilizers and pesticides would be necessary. There would be far less demand on scarce water, fuel, and other resources. Giant feed lots, which result in much animal manure washing into streams and rivers, could be converted to more ecologically sound uses.

The aims of vegetarians and ecologists are similar: simplify our life styles, have regard for the earth and all forms of life, and hence live consistent with the knowledge that "the earth is the Lord's."

6

Judaism, Vegetarianism, and Peace

The Jewish tradition mandates a special obligation to work for peace. The Bible does not command that people merely love peace or merely seek peace but that they actively pursue peace. The rabbis of the Talmud state that there are many commandments that require a certain time and place for their performance, but with regard to peace, "seek peace and pursue it" (Ps. 34:15); you are to seek it in your own place and pursue it everywhere else.[1] The famous talmudic sage Hillel states that we should "be of the disciples of Aaron, loving peace and pursuing peace."[2]

On the special duty of Jews to work for peace, the sages comment: "Said the Holy one blessed be He: The whole Torah is peace and to whom do I give it? To the nation who lives peace!"[3]

The rabbis of the Talmud use lavish words of praise to indicate the significance of peace:

> Great is peace, for God's name is peace. . . . Great is peace, for it encompasses all blessings. . . . Great is peace, for even in times of war, peace must be sought. . . . Great is peace seeing that when the Messiah is to come, He will commence with peace, as it is said, "How beautiful upon the mountains are the feet of the messenger of good tidings, that announce peace" (Isa. 52:7).[4]

> If Israel should worship idols, but she be at peace, God had no power, in effect, over them.[5]

61

> The whole Torah was given for the sake of peace, and it is
> said, "all her paths are peace" (Prov. 3:17).[6]

The important Jewish prayers, the *Amidah* (*Sh'moneh Esrei*),
the kaddish, the priestly blessing, and the grace after meals, all
conclude with a prayer for peace.

The Jewish tradition does not mandate absolute pacifism,
or peace at any price. The Israelites often went forth to battle
and not always in defensive wars. But they always held to the
ideal of universal peace and yearned for the day when there
would be no more bloodshed or violence.

> *And they shall beat their swords into plowshares,*
> *And their spears into pruning hooks;*
> *Nation shall not lift up sword against nation,*
> *Neither shall they learn war any more.*
> *But they shall sit every man under his vine and*
> *   under his fig tree;*
> *And none shall make them afraid;*
> *For the mouth of the Lord of hosts has spoken.*
>
> (Mic. 4:3-4; Isa. 2:4)

Judaism teaches that violence and war result directly from
injustice:

> The sword comes into the world because of justice delayed,
> because of justice perverted, and because of those who render
> wrong decisions.[7]

The Hebrew word for war, *milchama,* is directly derived from
the word *locham,* which means both "to feed" as well as "to
wage war."[8] The Hebrew word for bread, *lechem,* comes from
the same root. This suggests that the lack of bread and the
search for sufficient food tempt people to make war. The seeds
of war are often found in the inability of a nation to provide
adequate food for its people. Hence the tremendous amounts of
grains fed to animals raised for slaughter, which could be used
to feed starving people, ·could be a prime cause for war.

G. S. Arundale, a speaker at the World Vegetarian Congress in India, discussed the relationship between the treatment of animals and war:

> Whenever I see a meat and fish-ridden dining table, I know that I am looking upon one of the seeds of war and hatred—a seed that develops into an ugly weed of atrocity. . . . When people ask me, "Is there likely to be a future war?" I answer, "Yes, until the animals are treated as our younger brothers."[9]

Senator Mark Hatfield of Oregon has stated:

> Hunger and famine will do more to destabilize this world; [they are] more explosive than all atomic weaponry possessed by the big powers. Desperate people do desperate things. . . . Nuclear fission is now in the hands of even the developing countries in many of which hunger and famine are most serious.[10]

Richard J. Barnet, a director of the Washington-based Institute for Policy Studies and author of *The Lean Years,* an analysis of resource scarcities, believes that by the end of the century the anger and despair of hungry people could lead to acts of terrorism and economic class wars.[11] He states that the increasing number of hungry, desperate people in the world will turn to violence.[12]

The relationship between the consumption of meat and war is dramatized by the following dialog from Plato's *Republic:*

> *. . . and there will be animals of many other kinds*
> *if people eat them.*
> *Certainly.*
> *And living in this way we shall have much greater*
> *need of physicians than before?*
> *Much greater.*
> *And the country which was enough to support the*
> *original inhabitants will be too small now, and*
> *not enough?*
> *Quite true.*

Then a slice of our neighbors' land will be wanted
by us for pasture and tillage, and they will want a
slice of ours, if, like ourselves, they exceed the
limit of necessity, and give themselves up to the
unlimited accumulation of wealth?
That, Socrates, will be inevitable.
And so, we shall go to war, Glaucon. Shall we not?
Most certainly, he replied.[13]

The prophet Isaiah (66:3) states, "He who kills an ox is like he who kills a person." There are several ways of interpreting this verse, from a vegetarian point of view:

(1) By eating animals, we are consuming the grain that fattened the animal, which could have been used to save human lives.

(2) The ox helps the farmer to plow the earth and grow food. Hence the killing of an ox leads to less production of food and hence more starvation.[14]

(3) When a person is ready to kill an animal for his pleasure or profit, he will be ready to kill another human being.

Many people relate the cruelty involved in slaughtering animals for food to cruelty to people and eventually to war. The Nobel Prize winning writer Isaac Bashevis Singer states, "If a man has the heart to cut the throat of a chicken or a calf, there is no reason he should not be willing to cut the throat of a man."[15] Prime Minister Shri Morarji Desai of India has said, "If I am entitled to kill a living creature for my pleasure or my nourishment, equally would somebody else be justified in killing me for his enjoyment or sustenance."[16] Rabbi Samson Raphael Hirsch states, "The boy who, in crude joy, finds delight in the convulsions of an injured beetle or the anxiety of a suffering animal will soon also be dumb toward human pain."[17]

As the following poem, *Song of Peace,* indicates, the vegetarian writer George Bernard Shaw felt that the killing of animals today logically leads to the killing of men on the battlefield tomorrow:

We are the living graves of murdered beasts,
Slaughtered to satisfy our appetites,
We never pause to wonder at our feasts,
If animals like men, can possibly have rights.
We pray on Sundays that we may have light,
To guide our foot-steps on the paths we tread,
We're sick of war, we do not want to fight,
The thought of it now fills our heart with dread,
And yet we gorge ourselves upon the dead.
Like carrion crows, we live and feed on meat,
Regardless of the suffering and pain
We cause by doing so. If thus we treat
Defenseless animals, for sport or gain,
How can we hope in this world to attain
The PEACE we say we are so anxious for?
We pray for it, o'er hecatombs of slain,
To God, while outraging the moral law,
Thus cruelty begets its offspring—War.[18]

The former prime minister of Burma, U Nu, stated:

> World peace, or any other kind of peace, depends greatly on
> the attitude of the mind. Vegetarianism can bring about the
> right mental attitude for peace. In this world of lusts and
> hatred, greed and anger, force and violence, vegetarianism
> holds forth a way of life which, if practiced universally, can
> lead to a better, juster, and more peaceful community of
> nations.[19]

Albert Einstein said:

> The vegetarian manner of living, by its purely physical effect
> on the human temperament, would most beneficially influence
> the lot of mankind.[20]

Pandit Shiv Sharma, a speaker at the 24th World Vegetarian
Congress commented:

> It is a fact of history that whenever populations have been
> massacred, women submitted to mass rape (as happened in
> East Bengal before the birth of Bangladesh) and cities sacked
> and destroyed by fire and sword, it has never been done by
> a group of vegetarians.[21]

Isadora Duncan summarized many of the previous statements as follows:

> Who loves this terrible thing called war? Probably the meat eaters, having killed, feel the need to kill. . . . The butcher with his bloody apron incites bloodshed, murder. Why not? From cutting the throat of a young calf to cutting the throats of our brothers and sisters is but a step. While we ourselves are living graves of murdered animals, how can we expect any ideal conditions on the earth?[22]

Just as scarcity of food can lead to war, so can scarcity of sources of energy. A prime current threat to peace is the necessity of affluent countries to obtain sufficient oil to keep their economies running smoothly. The Persian Gulf area, where much of the world's oil is produced, is a place where there has been much recent instability and competition among the superpowers, which could result in war.

Meat-centered diets contribute to the energy crisis. It takes nearly 10 calories of fossil fuel energy to produce 1 calorie of food energy in the average American diet.[23] The main contributors to this are feedlot cattle raising and deep-sea fishing, which are very energy-intensive. It takes about 77 calories of fossil fuel energy to put 1 meat calorie on the plate.[24]

Feeding people rather than factory-bred animals requires far less irrigation, fertilizer, pesticides, mechanization, refrigeration, and processing, all of which consume much energy. The tremendous effects that meat-centered diets have on energy consumption can be seen in this example: if all the petroleum reserves in the world were devoted solely to feeding a typical North American diet to the world's more than 4 billion people, all the world's oil would be used in only 13 years.[25]

Judaism emphasizes the pursuit of justice and harmonious relations between nations to reduce violence and the prospects for war. The Prophet Isaiah states:

> And the work of righteousness shall be peace; And the effect of righteousness quietness and confidence forever. (Isa. 32:17)

The Psalmist writes,

> When loving-kindness and truth have met together, then righteousness and peace have kissed each other. (Ps. 85:11)

By adopting a diet that shows concern and loving-kindness for the hungry people of the world, by working for righteousness through more equitable sharing of God's abundant harvests, Jews and other people can play a significant role in moving the world toward that day when "nations shall not learn war any more."

7

Questions and Answers

Question 1. Don't Jews have to eat meat on the Sabbath and to enhance a *simcha* (joyous event)?

Answer. Rabbi Yehudah, known as the Prince, one of the outstanding sages of the talmudic period, states that the obligation to eat meat for rejoicing only applied at the time when the Temple was in existence.[1] He adds that after the destruction of the Temple one should rejoice with wine. Based on this, Rabbi Yishmael states, "From the day that the Holy Temple was destroyed, it would have been right to have imposed upon ourselves a law prohibiting the eating of flesh."[2] The reason that the rabbis did not make such a law was that they felt that most Jews were not ready to accept it. (It was also thought then that meat was necessary for proper nutrition.)

In *a responsa,* which is an answer to a question based on Jewish law, Rabbi Moshe Halevi Steinberg of Kiryat Yam, Israel, states, "One whose soul rebels against eating living things can without any doubt fulfill the commandment of enhancing the Sabbath and rejoicing on festivals by eating vegetarian foods. . . . Each person should delight in the Sabbath according to his own sensibility, enjoyment, and outlook."[3]

Eating meat is pleasurable only to those who crave it. It is a distress and torment to those who loathe it. Thus, the reverse of the argument applies: it is sinful for such people to suffer distress by eating flesh on the Sabbath.

Can sensitive, compassionate people enhance a joyous occasion by eating meat knowing that for their pleasure animals are cruelly treated, that grains are fed to animals while millions starve, and that their health is being impaired?

Question 2. If Jews don't eat meat, they'll be deprived of the opportunity to do many *mitzvot* (commandments). If God did not want meat to be eaten, why did he give so many laws concerning the slaughter, preparation, and consumption of meat?

Answer. As indicated previously, Rabbi Kook states that God provided many laws and regulations related to meat as a scolding, as a reminder that animals' lives are being destroyed, and in the hope that this would eventually lead people to vegetarianism.[4] He and others say that vegetarianism is the Jewish ideal diet and that God permitted meat eating as a concession, with many regulations designed to keep alive a sense of reverence for life.

There are other cases where laws were provided to regulate things that God would prefer people not to do. For example, God wishes people to live at peace, but he provides commandments related to war, because he knows that human beings tend to quarrel and seek victories over others. Similarly, the laws in the Torah related to slavery are a concession to human weakness.

By not eating meat, Jews are directly or indirectly acting consistently with many *mitzvot* and Jewish concepts, such as showing compassion to animals, preserving health, not wasting, feeding the hungry, and preserving the earth. Also, by not eating meat, a Jew cannot violate many possible prohibitions of the Torah, such as mixing meat and milk, eating nonkosher animals, and eating blood or fat.

Question 3. Judaism considers it an *averah* (sin) not to take advantage of the pleasurable things that God has put on the earth. As he put animals on the earth and it is pleasurable to eat them, is it not an *averah* to refrain from eating meat?

Answer. Can eating meat be pleasurable to a religious person when he or she knows that as a result health is endangered,

grain is wasted, and animals are being cruelly treated? There are
many other ways to gain pleasure without doing harm to living
creatures. The prohibition against abstaining from pleasurable
things only applies when there is no plausible basis for the
abstention; in the case of vegetarians, they abstain because of a
feeling that eating meat is injurious to health or because their
soul rebels at eating a living creature.

There are other cases in Judaism where pleasurable things
are forbidden or discouraged, such as the use of tobacco, drinking
liquor to excess, and sexual relations out of wedlock.

Question 4. Weren't people given dominion over the animals? Didn't God put them here for our use?

Answer. Dominion does not mean that we have the right to
conquer and exploit. Immediately after God gave people
dominion over animals (Gen. 1:26), he prohibited their use for
food (Gen. 1:29). Dominion means guardianship or stewardship—being co-workers with God in taking care of and improving
the world.[5]

The Talmud interprets "dominion" as the privilege of using
animals for labor only.[6] It is extremely doubtful that the concept
of dominion permits breeding animals and treating them as
machines designed solely to meet our needs.

Rabbi Kook states that dominion does not in any way imply
the rule of a haughty despot who tyrannically governs for his
own personal selfish ends and with a stubborn heart.[7] He states
that he cannot believe that such a repulsive form of servitude
could be forever sealed in the world of God whose "tender
mercies are over all His works."[8]

Rabbi Hirsch stresses that people have not been given the
right or the power to have all subservient to them. In commenting on Genesis 1:26, he states, "The earth and its creatures may
have other relationships of which we are ignorant, in which they
serve their own purpose."[9] Thus, above people's control over
nature there is a divine control to serve God's purposes and
objectives, and people have no right to interfere. Hence, people,
according to Judaism, do not have an unlimited right to use and
abuse animals and other parts of nature.

Question 5. If God wanted us to have vegetarian diets and not harm animals, why were the Temple sacrificial services established?

Answer. The sacrifices were not of Jewish origin. During the time of Moses, it was the general practice among all nations to worship by means of sacrifice.[10] There were many associated idolatrous practices. The great Jewish philosopher Maimonides states that God did not command the Israelites to give up and discontinue all these manners of service because "to obey such a commandment would have been contrary to the nature of man, who generally cleaves to that to which he is used."[11] For this reason, God allowed Jews to make sacrifices, but "He transferred to His service that which had served as a worship of created beings and of things imaginary and unreal."[12] All elements of idolatry were removed. Maimonides concludes:

> By this divine plan it was effected that the traces of idolatry were blotted out, and the truly great principle of our Faith, the Existence and Unity of God, was firmly established; this result was thus obtained without deterring or confusing the minds of the people by the abolition of the service to which they were accustomed and which alone was familiar to them.[13]

The Jewish philosopher Abarbanel reinforces Maimonides's argument. He cites a *Midrash* that indicated that the Jews had become accustomed to sacrifices in Egypt. To wean them from these idolatrous practices, God tolerated the sacrifices but commanded that they be offered in one central sanctuary.[14]

In his commentary on the sacrifices, Rabbi Hertz, the late chief rabbi of England, quotes Abarbanel:

> Thereupon the Holy One, blessed be He, said "Let them at all times offer their sacrifices before Me in the Tabernacle, and they will be weaned from idolatry, and thus be saved."[15]

Rabbi Hertz states that if Moses had not instituted sacrifices, which were admitted by all to have been the universal expression of religious homage, his mission would have failed and Judaism would have disappeared.[16] With the destruction of the Temple, the rabbis state that prayer and good deeds took the place of sacrifice.

Many Jewish scholars such as Rabbi Kook believe that animal sacrifices will not be reinstated in messianic times, even with the reestablishment of the Temple.[17] They believe that at that time human conduct will have advanced to such high standards that there will no longer be need for animal sacrifices to atone for sins. Only nonanimal sacrifices (grains, for example) to express gratitude to God would remain. There is a *Midrash* (teaching based on Jewish values and tradition) that states: "In the Messianic era, all offerings will cease, except the thanksgiving offering, which will continue forever."[18] This seems consistent with the belief of Rabbi Kook and others, based on the prophecy of Isaiah (11:6-9), that people and animals will be vegetarian in that time, and "none shall hurt nor destroy in all My Holy mountain."

Sacrifices, especially animal sacrifices, were not the primary concern of God. As a matter of fact, they could be an abomination to Him if not carried out together with deeds of loving kindness and justice. Consider these words of the prophets, the spokesmen of God:

What I want is mercy, not sacrifice. (Hos. 6:6)

"To what purpose is the multitude of your sacrifices unto Me?" sayeth the Lord. "I am full of the burnt offerings of rams, and the fat of fed beasts; and I delight not in the blood of bullocks, or of lambs or of he-goats . . . bring no more vain oblations. . . . Your new moon and your appointed feasts my soul hateth; . . . and when ye spread forth your hands, I will hide mine eyes from you; yea, when ye make many prayers, I will not hear; your hands are full of blood." (Isa. 1:11-16)

I hate, I despise your feasts, and I will take no delight in your solemn assemblies. Yea, though you offer me burnt-offerings and your meal offerings, I will not accept them, neither will I regard the peace-offerings of your fat beasts. Take thou away from me the noise of thy song; and let Me

not hear the melody of thy psalteries. But let justice well up
as waters, and righteousness as a mighty stream. (Amos 5:21-4)

Deeds of compassion and kindness toward all creation are of
greater significance to God than sacrifices: "To do charity and
justice is more acceptable to the Lord than sacrifice" (Prov.
21:3).

Question 6. Don't the laws of *shechita* provide for a
humane slaughter of animals so that we need not be concerned
with violations of *tsa'ar ba'alei chayim?*

Answer. It is true that *shechita* has been found in scientific
tests conducted in the United States and other countries to be
a relatively painless method of slaughter.[19] But can we consider
only the final minutes of an animal's life? What about the tremendous pain and cruelty involved in the entire process of
raising and transporting animals? When, as was shown in chapter 3, the consumption of meat is not necessary and is even
harmful to people's health can any method of slaughter be considered humane? Is this not a contradiction in terms?

No book on Judaism and vegetarianism can be considered
complete without a discussion of the very controversial subject
of shackling and hoisting. It is very important to realize that
shackling and hoisting are preparatory to *shechita,* not part of
shechita. Shackling and hoisting are a method of bringing a con-
scious animal, as required by Jewish law, to the *shochet* for
slaughter. They are a means of restraining the animal and posi-
tioning it for the ritual kill.

Prior to the introduction of shackling and hoisting, the general
method of restraint was that of casting the animal to the floor
where it was held in place for *shechita.* In 1906, the U. S. Department of Agriculture ruled that this process was unsanitary because a diseased animal could infect all other animals that might
come into contact with its blood. Thus the Department of Agriculture ordered that all animals must be lifted off the packing-
house floor prior to slaughter,[20] requiring the process of shackling
and hoisting, which is *not* an indigenous part of the ritual of
shechita.

The problem with shackling and hoisting is that they cause great pain to animals and thus violate the Jewish mandate of *tsa'ar ba'alei chayim*. The process involves placing an iron chain around the hind leg or legs of the animal and hoisting the animal into the air by its hind legs while the rest of the body and head are suspended downward. Even in the comparatively short period in which the animal hangs from its leg or legs, it experiences great pain.[21]

Fortunately, there is an alternative, more humane method that is acceptable to Jewish law. Holding pens have been developed to meet the requirements of ritual slaughter and the Department of Agriculture law, while avoiding the use of shackling and hoisting. These pens have been endorsed by the Jewish Joint Advisory Committee on *Shechita,* the Rabbinical Council of America, and several prominent orthodox rabbis.[22]

Because of their high initial cost, many slaughterhouses have not adopted the holding pens. However, the use of the pens would save slaughterhouses money after a few years because shackling and hoisting sometimes damage the animals and make the meat unkosher.

Many humane groups have pushed for legislation banning shackling and hoisting. Unfortunately, some antisemitic groups have used the issue to discredit *shechita* as well as Jewish law in general. It is very important that the Jewish community work for humane alternatives to shackling and hoisting, primarily to be consistent with the mandate to avoid *tsa'ar ba'alei chayim* but also to reduce criticism. Of course, as indicated earlier, the best way to be consistent with Jewish teachings concerning animals is to be a vegetarian.

Question 7. What is the definition of a vegetarian diet? Can a vegetarian eat fish?

Answer. The generally accepted definition of a vegetarian diet is that it includes no flesh foods, that is, no meat, poultry, or fish.[23] There are three types of vegetarian diets: the lacto-ovo-vegetarian diet, which includes dairy products and eggs; the lacto-vegetarian diet, which includes dairy products but not eggs;

and the vegan (pronounced "vee-gan") diet, which uses no dairy products or eggs.[24] Vegans frequently do not use honey and avoid using non-food animal products such as leather, wool, and fur. They base their practice on a belief that it is ethically wrong to kill animals or exploit them in any way.

Contrary to some people's beliefs, fish cannot be included in a vegetarian diet. Vegetarians avoid fish because they feel it is unnecessary to destroy living creatures for food that is not necessary for proper nutrition; the extensive pollution of many bodies of water and the magnification of pollution effects through food chains makes the consumption of fish dangerous to health. Potential dangers in breast feeding because of chemicals and pesticides in mothers' milk, primarily owing to the consumption of meat and fish, have already been discussed.[25]

Question 8. I enjoy eating meat. Why should I give it up?

Answer. If one is solely motivated by what will bring pleasure, then perhaps this question cannot be answered. But Judaism is concerned with far more: doing *mitzvot,* performing good deeds, sanctifying occasions, helping feed the hungry, pursuing justice and peace, and so on. The objective in writing this book is to indicate that people who take such Jewish values seriously should become vegetarians.

Even if one is primarily motivated by considerations of pleasure and convenience, the negative health effects of a meat-centered diet should be taken into account. One cannot enjoy life when one is not in good health.

Question 9. What if everyone became vegetarian? Wouldn't animals overrun the earth?

Answer. This concern is based on an insufficient understanding of animal behavior, both natural and under present factory conditions. There are not millions of turkeys around at Thanksgiving because they want to help celebrate the holiday but because farmers want them to be. The breeders, not the animals themselves, control the breeding behavior and thus the number of stock. Recent studies have shown that animals, in natural conditions, adjust their numbers to fit their environment and food supply. An end to the distortion of the sex lives of animals to suit our needs would lead to a drop, rather than an increase, in animals.[26]

Note that we are not overrun by the animals that we do not eat, such as lions, elephants, and crocodiles. The problem often is that of the extinction of animals, rather than their overrunning the earth. There are many meat-bearing animals today because they are raised under rigid breeding control.

What would happen to butchers, *shochets,* and others dependent for a livelihood on the consumption of meat?

There could be a shift from the production of flesh products to that of nutritious vegetarian dishes. In England during World War II, when there was a shortage of meat, butchers relied mainly on the sale of fruits and vegetables.

The change to vegetarianism would probably be gradual. This would provide time for a transition to other jobs. Some of the funds saved by individuals and groups because of lower food and health costs should be used to provide incomes for people during the retraining period.

The same kind of question can be asked about other moral issues. What would happen to all the arms merchants if we had universal peace? What would happen to doctors and nurses if people took better care of themselves, stopped smoking, improved their diets, and so on? Immoral or inefficient practices should not be supported by pointing out that some people earn a living from them.

Question 10. Weren't the Jewish sages aware of the evils related to eating meat? If so, why does so much of talmudic literature discuss laws and customs related to the consumption of meat? Are you suggesting that Judaism has been morally wrong in not advocating vegetarianism?

Answer. Conditions today differ greatly from those in biblical times and throughout most of Jewish history. Only recently has strong medical evidence linked a meat-centered diet with many types of disease. Modern farming methods lead to conditions quite different from those that prevailed previously. To produce meat today, animals are treated very cruelly, they are fed tremendous amounts of grains while millions of people starve, and there are many problems related to pollution and resource scarcities. When it was felt that eating meat was necessary for health and the many negative conditions related to intensive raising of animals did not exist, the Jewish sages were not morally wrong in not advocating vegetarianism.

Question 11. Because the majority of Jews will probably continue to eat meat, isn't it better that they do so without being aware of the Jewish principles such as *bal tashchit, tsa'ar ba'alei chayim,* and *pikuach nefesh* that are being violated? Shouldn't a Jewish vegetarian abstain from meat quietly and not try to convert others to his type of diet?

Answer. This is a common attitude that the author has found. People feel that if there are benefits to vegetarianism and if some people want to have such a diet, fine. But they should keep it to themselves and not try to convert others.

The question really becomes one of how seriously we take Jewish values. Are we to ignore the Torah mandates to preserve our health, show compassion for animals, not waste, help feed the hungry, preserve the earth, and many others that are violated directly or indirectly by a meat-centered diet? Is it correct that people be kept uninformed about the many violations of Torah law so that they can continue their eating habits with a clear conscience?

Judaism teaches that one should try to teach others and assist them to carry out commandments. A Hasidic teacher concludes:

> Man, the master of choice, shall say: "Only for my sake was the whole world created!" Therefore every man shall be watchful and strive to redeem the world and supply that wherein it is lacking, at all times and in all places.[27]

The importance of speaking out when improper actions are occurring is indicated by the following powerful talmudic teaching:

Whoever is able to protest against the transgression of his own family and does not do so is punished for the transgressions of his family. Whoever is able to protest against the transgressions of the people of his community and does not do so is punished for the transgressions of his community. Whoever is able to protest against the transgression of the entire world and does not do so is punished for the transgressions of the entire world.[28]

The Talmud also relates a story of how apparently righteous individuals were punished along with the wicked because "they had the power to protest but they did not."[29]

Related to these principles are the following teachings of the Jewish sages:

> If a man of learning participates in public affairs and serves as judge or arbiter, he gives stability to the land. But if he sits in his home and says to himself, "What have the affairs of society to do with me? . . . Why should I trouble myself with the people's voices of protest? Let my soul dwell in peace!" If he does this, he overthrows the world.[30]
>
> If the community is in trouble, a man must not say, "I will go to my house, and eat and drink, and peace shall be with thee, O my soul." But a man must share in the trouble of his community, even as Moses did. He who shares in its troubles is worthy to see its consolation.[31]

Question 12. How would a Jewish vegetarian celebrate Passover?

Answer. Today there is no need to eat or cook meat on Passover. The eating of the Pascal lamb is no longer required now that the Temple has been destroyed. One is required to commemorate this act not to participate in it. The late Dayan Feldman stated that mushrooms, which have a fleshy appearance, can be used on the seder plate to commemorate the Pascal lamb.[32] The Talmud indicates that a broiled beet can be used.[33]

The proper celebration of Passover requires the absence of leaven and the use of unleavened bread, which we are commanded to eat "throughout your generations." There are many vegetarian recipes that are appropriate for seders and other Passover meals.

Because Passover is the celebration of our redemption from slavery, we should also consider freeing ourselves from the slavery to harmful eating habits. As our homes are freed from leaven, perhaps we should also free our bodies from harmful foods. Because Passover is a time of regeneration, physical as well as spiritual, the maximum use should be made of raw fruits and vegetables, which have cleansing properties.

There are other Passover themes related to vegetarian ideas. The call at the seders for "all who are hungry to come and eat" can be a reminder that our diets can be a factor in reducing global starvation. The Passover theme of freedom can be related to the horrible conditions of slavery under which animals are raised today.

Question 13. In Jewish literature, it is stated that with the advent of the Messiah a banquet will be given by God to the righteous at which the flesh of the giant fish, leviathan, will be served.[34] Isn't this inconsistent with the idea that the messianic period will be vegetarian?

Answer. These legends concerning the leviathan are interpreted as allegories by all the commentators, with the exception of some who are very conservative.[35] According to Maimonides, the banquet is an allusion to the spiritual enjoyment of the intellect.[36] Abarbanel and others consider the expressions about the leviathan to be allusions to the destruction of the powers that are hostile to the Jews.[37]

Question 14. Won't a movement by Jews toward vegetarianism mean less emphasis on *kashrut* (the Jewish kosher laws) and eventually a disregard of these laws?

Answer. Not necessarily. One of the purposes of the laws of *kashrut* is to keep alive a reverence for life. This is certainly consistent with vegetarianism. Another purpose is to avoid pagan practices, which often involve much cruelty to animals and people. This too is certainly consistent with vegetarian ideals.

In many ways becoming a vegetarian makes it easier and

cheaper to observe the laws of *kashrut;* this might attract many new adherents to keeping kosher and eventually to other important Jewish values. As a vegetarian, one need not be concerned with separate dishes, mixing *milchigs* (dairy products) with *fleichigs* (meat products), waiting 3 or 6 hours after eating meat before being allowed to eat dairy products, storing four sets (two for regular use and two for Passover use) of dishes, silverware, pots, and pans, and many other considerations that must concern the nonvegetarian who wishes to observe *kashrut* strictly. In addition, a vegetarian is in no danger of eating blood or fat, which are prohibited, or the flesh of a nonkosher animal. It should be noted that being a vegetarian does not automatically guarantee that one will maintain the laws of *kashrut* as, for example, certain baked goods and cheeses may not be kosher. When in doubt, of course, a trusted rabbinic authority should be consulted.

Many people today reject *kashrut* because of the high costs involved. A person can obtain proper nourishment at far lower costs with a vegetarian diet. In this period of inflation and other economic problems, this may prevent the loss of many *kashrut* observers.

In a personal letter to the author, Rabbi Robert Gordis, Professor of Bible at the Jewish Theological Seminary, indicates that he sees little hope that *kashrut* will be maintained by most Jewish people in our day in its present form. He indicates that vegetarianism, the logical consequence of Jewish teaching, would be a way of protecting *kashrut*. He states, "Vegetarianism offers an ideal mode for preserving the religious and ethical values which *kashrut* was designed to concretize in human life."

There are several examples in Jewish history when a change to vegetarianism enabled Jews to adhere to *kashrut*. As indicated earlier, Daniel and his companions were able to avoid eating nonkosher food by adopting a vegetarian diet. The historian Josephus relates how some Jewish priests on trial in Rome ate only figs and nuts to avoid eating flesh that had been used in idol worship.[38] Some Maccabees, during the struggles against the Syrians, escaped to the mountains where they lived on only plant foods to avoid "being polluted like the rest" (2 Mac. 5:27).

Question 15. Instead of advocating vegetarianism, shouldn't we try to alleviate the evils of the factory farming system so that animals are treated better, less grain is wasted, and less health-harming chemicals are used?

Answer. The breeding of animals is a big business, whose prime concern is profit. Animals are raised the way they are today because it increases profits. Improving conditions as suggested by this question would certainly be a step in the right direction, but it would be strongly resisted by the meat industry and, if successful, would greatly increase already high prices.

Here are two counter questions. Why not abstain from eating meat as a protest against present policies while trying to improve them? Even under the best of conditions, why take the life of a creature of God, "whose tender mercies are over all His creatures," when it is not necessary for proper nutrition?

Question 16. Isn't a movement toward vegetarianism a movement away from Jewish traditions with regard to diet? Isn't there a danger that once some traditions are changed, others may readily follow, and little will be left of Judaism as we have known it?

Answer. Jewish law is based on a two-part structure: written law (the Jewish Bible) and oral law (Talmud, *responsa* literature, and other rabbinic writings). Although the written law remains the unchanging base, the oral law is constantly adapting to current conditions. This system has kept Judaism as alive and applicable today as it was centuries ago. In contemporary times, the vast *responsa* literature of this century has enabled new traditions to form within *halachic* bounds.

A move toward vegetarianism is actually a return to Jewish traditions, to taking Jewish values seriously. A movement toward vegetarianism can help revitalize Judaism. It can show that Jewish values still are taken seriously and can be applied to help solve current world problems related to hunger, waste, and pollution. This could help attract idealist Jews. Hence, rather than a movement away from Jewish traditions, it would have the opposite effect.

Question 17. Aren't there also problems related to eating

vegetables? Don't vegetables have feelings? Aren't vegetables also sprayed with chemicals?

Answer. The concept of kindness to plants is actually a strong positive point for vegetarianism. Because animals have to eat about ten times as much vegetable food to return a single unit of food value as meat, a vegetarian diet means less destruction of plants. Also, most vegetarian food can be obtained without killing the plant; this includes ripe fruits and nuts, berries, melons, seeds, legumes, tomatos, squash, cucumbers, and pumpkins.

It is good that people are starting to realize that plants have a certain state of consciousness. Perhaps this will lead to a greater awareness that animals are not unfeeling beasts. And certainly the consciousness in plants is of a different quality than that in humans and animals.

Unfortunately, it is true that vegetables are sprayed with many chemicals. It is important to wash them well. Also, efforts should be made to reduce unnecessary spraying of pesticides. But here, too, vegetarianism is beneficial because, as indicated previously, the movement of chemicals up the food chain leads to far greater amounts of pollutants in meat and fish.

Vegetarians, especially those who have recently changed their diets, are generally on the defensive. They must deal with many questions, such as the ones in this chapter. Those who eat meat have the support of society, and thus they never consider the consequences of their diet. Hence it is vegetarians who are asked to explain the reasons for their diet, rather than those who support the brutal treatment and unnecessary slaughter of animals that a meat-centered diet requires.

Perhaps there are times when vegetarians should take the offensive in conversations with meat eaters. To that end, responses to questions can be used to teach others basic ideas, which can help show the benefits of vegetarianism and its consistency with Jewish values.

Here are some questions that can help to turn the tables on nonvegetarians: Do you know about the cruelty related to raising animals for food today? Are you aware of the links between meat eating and heart disease, cancer, and other illnesses? Could you visit a slaughterhouse or kill an animal yourself? Do you know that while millions die annually of starvation most grain grown in the United States and other affluent countries is fed to animals? Are you aware of the consequences of a meat-centered diet with regard to pollution, use of land, water, and other resources, and the increased potential for violence and war? Do you know that vegetarianism is the diet most consistent with Jewish values?

8

B'Tay-Avon:
Have a Hearty Appetite!

(Contributed by Dr. Shoshana Margolin)

People who consider adopting a vegetarian life-style—whether for health reasons or ethics invariably ask:
"What will I eat?" "Where will I get my protein?" "Will I go through life with a feeling of deprivation and not being full?"
Nothing will answer these questions more positively than delicious, nourishing and well-planned vegetarian meals. This chapter gives guidelines that can ease initiation into this new world of "harmless eating"—harmless to your own health and harmless because there is no bloodshed involved.
Consider the aesthetics: you walk into a butcher shop, you see the bleeding carcasses hanging on hooks and parts of animal bodies being cut, weighed, and chopped. You notice the blood-stained apron and hands of the butcher. You smell the odor of death, of decomposing flesh. All these are very appetizing to a lion, whose constitution is suited for this fare, but most people—yes, even meat eaters—find it positively repulsive or at least unappealing. The average homemaker may repress these feelings because by custom a trip to the butcher is a necessity to be tolerated in order to feed the family; yet when a woman is pregnant

and her body reactions are intensified, she will likely defer trips to the butcher due to nausea.

To be made appetizing, meat must be softened by cooking and the smell and taste disguised with spices and vegetables. When we poll meat eaters at random and ask if they would eat meat provided they had to slaughter animals themselves, we discover many vegetarians-at-heart. The act of preying and tearing flesh is appropriate only for animals with claws and fangs, the carnivorous animals. Most people would *not* enjoy a trip to the slaughterhouse; many shudder at the sight of suffering.

Compare the butcher shop or slaughterhouse with the sight of fruits and vegetables displayed for sale—the lively colors of red, green, yellow, orange, and purple, the aroma of oranges, of ripe peaches, of Golden Delicious apples, of ripe bananas! Don't you find it appetizing just the way it is? Wouldn't you eat fruit even if you had to pick your own? The answers to these questions would be very different from answers to equivalent questions at the butcher shop. Most people *enjoy* picking fruit, vegetables, and berries. They *enjoy* spending time on a fruit farm. They may even note the perfect fit between their palms and the shape of the fruit, as if these were designed for each other.

When you think of it—even without considering the strong evidence of Comparative Anatomy—it makes sense that a species of creatures will find *appetizing* to its senses (sight, smell, touch, and taste) those foods that are suited for it by original design. To illustrate this point, monkeys find bananas naturally appealing as is, or else they would not eat them. So it is with other animals: they need not go to school to learn their natural diet; their senses tell them! They don't disguise the flavor by cooking, broiling, baking, sautéing, steaming, marinating, or by using spice or smoke. They love their food naturally just the way it is! We humans, however, have gotten so far from our source (perhaps the expulsion from the Garden of Eden had a deep dietary significance!) that many of us have lost our instincts completely or at least aberrated them. Our distorted perceptions are clearly depicted by the prophet Isaiah: "'Woe unto them that call evil

good, and good evil . . . that change bitter into sweet and sweet
into bitter." (Isaiah 5:20)

Let us regain our senses so that we no longer allow cancer-
causing junk food to be labeled "kosher" but return this word
to its *complete* original meaning—"fit to eat." It is time for us
to expand our consciousness by returning to the natural diet for
which our bodies were designed and to reap the many rewards.

A. A WAY OF LIFE

Vegetarianism is relevant only when practiced. If it includes
orientation to better health, it will probably be practiced longer
(as healthy habits have a definite effect on life span).

Some suggestions for making the transition to vegetarianism
and a healthier life-style easier follow. (Remember, you know
yourself best; adopt suggestions and pace of change most comfortable for you.)

(1) It may be advisable to adopt a vegetarian life-style in
small, graduated steps, according to individual prefer-
ence.

(2) It is important to supply your nutritional needs by eating a wide variety of foods in season rather than to
depend on a limited selection of foods with which you
were previously familiar. Experiment with new foods;
dare to improvise! When using God's bounty in natural
form, you can't make serious mistakes.

(3) Plan menus in advance. Take time to build attractive
meals using foods you enjoy. Besides recipes given
later in this chapter, you can find good vegetarian
recipes in the *Jewish Vegetarian* and in books listed
in the bibliography. Generally aim to have simple meals
with quick and easy preparation. Simplicity in diet has
many advantages, including health and saving time.

(4) Approach each meal with positive expectations. Enjoy
your food. Don't consider yourself an ascetic. Realize

that your diet is best for life—your life and that of spared animals, hungry people, and the environment.

(5) Learn principles of sound nutrition. Read books on vegetarianism and natural health. Start to build a home library that you can use to look up questions as well as to lend books to friends. Subscribe to health magazines, such as *Health Science, Ahimsa, Vegetarian Voice, Prevention, Let's Live, Vegetarian Times, Bestways* and *East West Journal.* Attend vegetarian and natural health meetings and conferences.

(6) Become familiar with vegetarian restaurants in your area. The *Annual Directory of Vegetarian Restaurants* is available from Daystar Publishing Company, P.O. Box 707, Angwin, CA 94508. Find out which restaurants offer salad bars with a wide variety of fresh vegetables. If you observe laws of *kashrut,* check a restaurant's acceptability.

(7) Associate with other vegetarians and become friendly with health-minded people for mutual support and reinforcement. This is valuable even if socialization is mostly by telephone. It is especially important for children—they must know that there are others like them.

(8) Become familiar with local health food stores. Here are some special items that you should get to know:

- Tamari—a natural soy sauce prepared without caramel coloring or chemicals.
- Tahini—natural sesame butter. (*Erewhon* is a good brand.)
- Tofu—soy bean curd, which is a high-protein product that can be adapted to many vegetarian dishes.
- Rice cakes—puffed brown rice pressed to form round cakes, which are crisp and crunchy.
- Unsulfured dried fruits.
- Unsalted shelled nuts and seeds.

The following equipment may be very valuable in preparing food: a vegetable juicer and a stainless steel steamer (with perforated "wings" that open to any size pot and three legs, so water does not touch the vegetables).

(9) Increase consumption of fruits, vegetables, and their freshly squeezed juices. See to it that a good variety of these foods, as well as seeds, raisins, and nuts, are always available at home.

(10) The vegetable kingdom is the ultimate source of all protein. The many nonmeat sources of protein include grains (corn, wheat, rice, oats, barley, millet, etc.), legumes (peas, lentils, soybeans, kidney beans, garbanzos, etc.), dairy products (milk, cheese, yogart, etc.), and the many types of nuts and seeds. By mixing compatible foods, the value of the protein is enhanced. This is known as complementary protein and is discussed in detail in *Diet for a Small Planet* by Frances Lappe.

(11) Use healthier substitutes: Instead of polished rice, use brown rice. Instead of white flour, use whole wheat or brown rice meal. Instead of sugar or an artificial sweetener, use honey, rice bran syrup, or blackstrap molasses. Instead of chocolate or cocoa, use carob powder. Instead of margerine, use sesame oil (in recipes) or Tahini dressing as a spread. Instead of commercial oils, use sesame oil or olive oil.

(12) When you are invited to a wedding, bar mitzvah, or dinner at someone's home, let your hosts know beforehand that you eat only vegetarian food. Generally, they comply cordially. If they ask, "why?," use this as an opportunity to educate them, using the concepts in this and other vegetarian books.

(13) Some additional valuable suggestions for healthy eating are:

- Become a label reader; pay special attention to small print on food packages. Minimize use of products with food colorings, preservatives, stabilizers and artificial flavors.
- Minimize and aim to avoid the use of foods that contain caffeine, such as coffee, cola drinks, chocolate, and regular tea (as well as drugs).
- Minimize use of salt, sugar, and artificial sweeteners.
- Try to avoid use of aluminum cookware and "silver" foil (which is really aluminum foil). The best cookware to use is Pyrex, Corningware, enamel (if not chipped), and stainless steel, in this order.
- Minimize frying.

These suggestions are just a beginning. As you read, attend meetings and interact with like-minded individuals, you will expand your horizons and find the life-style ideal for you.

B. RECIPES

Ideally, a vegetarian diet should not contain canned products, refined sugar and flour, salt, or even cooked foods. However, when you first adopt a vegetarian diet, you may not wish to give up all of these immediately. Some of the following recipes take this into account.

COMPLETE PROTEIN CASSEROLES

We start with a wide variety of vegetarian complete protein casseroles which can be obtained by combining ingredients from each of the five columns in the table below. A total of almost 8,000 different casseroles can be made, enough to last you over twenty years, if you use one each day!

TABLE II

Ingredients for Complete Protein Casseroles[a]

Column 1[b]	Column 2[b]	Column 3	Column 4	Column 5
(2 cups cooked)	(1 cup cooked)	(Sauce: 1 can soup and ¾ cup water)	(Vegetables to make 1½ cup)	(3-5 Tbsp. topping)
Brown rice	Soybeans	Cream of tomato	Browned celery and green onions	Wheat germ
Macaroni, whole wheat	Lima beans	Cream of potato	Mushrooms and bamboo shoots	Slivered almonds
Corn	Peas	Cream of mushroom	Browned green pepper and garlic	Fresh whole wheat bread crumbs
Spaghetti, whole wheat	Kidney beans	Cream of celery	Cooked green beans	Sesame seeds
Brown rice	Black beans	Cheddar cheese soup	Cooked carrots	Brewer's yeast (debittered)
Noodles, whole wheat	Garbanzos (chickpeas)	Cream of pea	Browned onion and pimiento	Sunflower seeds

[a]Each casserole serves from 4 to 6 people.
[b]The ingredients in Columns 1 and 2 form complementary proteins.

(1) Choose one ingredient in the proportions noted, from each of the five columns.
(2) Mix together ingredients from first four columns.
(3) Pour into greased casserole dish (1 quart) and bake 30 minutes at 375°F.
(4) Top with one choice from column 5 and bake 15 minutes longer at 325°F.
(5) Salt to taste at the table. Serve with bread and a salad.

By picking one ingredient from each column in Table III, you can create over 260,000 different salad combinations, enough to last over 700 years if you use a different one each day. As you may choose more than one ingredient from each column, there are almost an infinite number of salad combinations.

MIX-MATCH SALAD GUIDE

TABLE III
Ingredients for Mix-Match Salads[a]

Greens (1½ cups)	Color (2 tbsp.)	Flavor (to taste)	Protein (2–4 oz.)	Texture (1 tbsp.)	Dressing (about ¼ cup)
Iceberg lettuce	Tomatoes	Cucumber slices	Cheese	Radishes	Mayonnaise
Romaine lettuce	Red cabbage	Raisins	Hard-cooked eggs	Carrot chunks	Creamy french
Boston lettuce	Diced red apples	Onion rings	Sunflower seeds	Croutons	Russian
Raw spinach	Red pepper	Sauerkraut	Tofu	Celery slices	Thousand Island
Chinese cabbage	Stuffed olives	Garlic (rub bowl)	Walnuts	Green peppers	Oil and tamari
Escarole	Black olives	Diced pickles	Cooked beans	Water chestnuts	Yogurt
Cabbage	Grated carrots	Watercress	Toasted almonds	Pretzel sticks	Sour cream
Chicory	Pickled beets	Chutney	Soy nuts	Sprouts	Blue cheese

[a]Use one or more ingredient from each column for each portion.

91

Basic Beginner Main Dishes

Loretta's Nutty Casserole

1 cup chopped nuts (peanuts
   or cashews)
1 cup chopped onion
1 cup chopped celery
1 cup chopped mushrooms

1 cup fine egg noodles
1 cup Chinese noodles
2 cups vegetable stock
   (or boullion)
2 tablespoons oil

Place oil in casserole dish. Mix all other ingredients. Bake, covered, for 1 hour at 350°F.

Vegetarian Nut Loaf

1½ cups chopped peanuts, walnuts,
    or cashews
2 grated carrots
2 cups finely sliced celery
1 cup chopped onion
¼ cup wheat germ
4 ounces mushrooms

1 cup whole wheat bread crumbs
3 eggs or ¾ cup egg substitute
1 cup chopped eggplant,
   cauliflower, or green beans
1 can condensed tomato or cream
   of mushroom soup, undiluted

Combine all ingredients, mixing thoroughly. Bake in greased loaf pan at 400°F for 1 hour, or until browned. If desired, sliced cheese may be melted on top during the last 20 minutes of baking.

Vegetable "Patties"

¼ cup oil
½ cup chopped onion
½ cup finely chopped celery
⅓ cup peanut butter
1 egg, well beaten
4 Idaho potatoes, cooked, peeled,
   and mashed or diced

1 cup cooked chopped carrots
   or peas
1½ cups flavored bread crumbs
   Oil for frying

In a skillet, heat oil and sauté onion and celery until tender (about 5 minutes). Pour into a bowl with drippings. Add peanut butter, potatoes, egg, and vegetables. Stir until well blended. Shape mixture into six patties. Roll patties in crumbs until completely coated. Brown patties on each side in shallow preheated oil (about 350°F) or on greased pan in oven (about 45 minutes). Drain on absorbent paper, if necessary.

VEGETARIAN "CHOPPED LIVER" I

1 very large onion	12 walnuts, grated in a blender
(or 2 medium)	2 cups cooked peas
2 tablespoons oil	8 hard-cooked eggs

Sauté lightly chopped onion in oil until browned. Mash eggs and add to peas, mixing until well blended. Add walnuts and onions and keep mashing until very well blended.

THE NILOGRAM APPROACH

During years of providing professional nutritional advice, the author of this chapter has found the Nilogram method of eating for health to be very valuable. (A comprehensive book on this method will be forthcoming.) Some of the most important principles of this system are the following:

(1) Eat fruits and vegetables at separate meals.

(2) Eat starch and protein at separate meals.

(3) Vegetables are compatible with either starch or protein.

(4) Any cooking or processing is a compromise on the ideal.

(5) Do not drink during or shortly after a meal (drink only before or between meals).

(6) When you observe food order and food combinations and chew your food well, you need not worry about quantities. Your body will tell you when to stop eating.

(7) At any meal, eat juicier foods before the concentrated, and raw before the cooked, if possible.

The following recipes are consistent with the Nilogram approach and are also valuable for a more general vegetarian diet.

NUT LOAF

4 tablespoons olive oil
1 cup grated carrots
1 cup chopped celery
½ cup chopped onion
1½ cups soya milk
¼ cup rice polish (or soy flour)
1 teaspoon salt

1 dash pepper (optional)
¼ teaspoon thyme
1 cup shredded cheddar cheese
1 cup chopped walnuts or pecans
¾ cup plain wheat germ
3 slightly beaten eggs

Sauté in oil, carrots, celery, and onion until tender. Meanwhile, combine in a blender soy milk, rice polish, salt, pepper, and thyme. Pour over the sautéd vegetables, cook, and stir over moderate heat until thick. Stir in cheddar cheese, nuts, and wheat germ. For a *pareve* (nondairy) loaf, use shredded firm tofu (soy curd) instead of cheese. Add 3 eggs and mix. Pour into 8×8×2 inch greased baking pan. Bake at 350°F for 40 minutes, or until brown and firm. Let cool a few minutes before slicing. Serve with Pareve Gravy (recipe given later) or onion sauce.

RICE PUDDING

1½ cups brown rice
3 cups water
2 beaten eggs
(optional)
1 cup raisins (presoaked)

2 grated apples
1 teaspoon cinnamon
apple juice or sesame butter
(optional)

Soak brown rice in water overnight. Then cook until soft. Add the remaining ingredients. Put into unwaxed paper bowls (or into muffin cup liners for smaller portions) and bake for 45 minutes at 350°F (or until brown on top).

MILLET PIE

1 cup millet
2½ cups water
2 grated zucchini
2 chopped onions

3 tablespoons olive oil
2 beaten eggs
1 teaspoon tamari (soy sauce)

Soak millet in water overnight. Then cook until soft (15-20 minutes). In skillet, sauté together zucchini and onions in olive oil. Add soy sauce plus herbal seasoning of your choice. Mix with eggs and bake in oiled 9-inch pie plate for 30 minutes at 350°F.

EGGPLANT SALAD

1 eggplant
½ tablespoon olive oil
½ tablespoon lemon juice
2 tablespoons plain tahini
   (unprepared)

¼ teaspoon salt or soy sauce
   (optional)

Wash eggplant. Pierce once with knife or fork (to allow heated air to escape when baking) and put in moderate oven for 40 minutes or longer (timing depends on the size of the eggplant). When fully baked, knife will go in very easily. Remove from oven, slit open, and scoop out the pulp. Mash with chopper. When cool, add olive oil, lemon juice, and tahini. Use your intuition and taste-test for proportions (*any* ratios turn out fine). Serve cold in a scoop on lettuce leaf, or as sandwich filling.

LENTIL SOUP

2 cups lentils
6 cups water
1 small whole onion
2 grated carrots
2 diced potatoes

1 tablespoon chopped celery
2 tablespoons chopped parsley
½ teaspoon salt
½ teaspoon tamari sauce

Soak washed lentils overnight in water. In the morning, cook with onion, carrots, potatoes, celery, and parsley. Season with salt or tamari (soy sauce). Remove onion before serving.

ZUCCHINI CREAM SOUP

2 diced onions	2 quarts water
1 tablespoon sesame oil	Spike (prepackaged
6 diced potatoes	combination of 39 spices,
4 diced zucchini	herbs, and flavorings)

Sauté onions in oil and set aside. Cook potatoes and zucchini in water until soft. Add Spike or other herbal seasoning and process all the ingredients in the blender until creamy. Serve immediately, with chopped parsley sprinkled on top.

SOYBURGER

2 mashed tofu cakes (bean curd)	1 clove minced garlic
1 large diced onion	½ teaspoon ground celery seed
1 tablespoon sesame oil	1 teaspoon soy sauce
1 beaten egg	wheat germ (approximate)

Sauté onion in oil. Add remaining ingredients, including enough wheat germ to hold the mix together. Form patties and bake on oiled pan in moderate oven for 30 minutes.

ARTICHOKE

1 artichoke	individual bowls of tahini dressing

Wash artichoke well by running tap water between the leaves. Cook whole (no need to cut or trim) in enough water to cover for about 30 minutes. Serve with tahini for dipping. Artichoke is eaten by tearing off one leaf at a time, dipping it in the tahini, and scraping the leaf between your teeth to extract the edible pulp.

TAHINI DRESSING

½ cup light-colored sesame butter
    (tahini)
¾ cup water
½ teaspoon Spike
¼ teaspoon paprika

¼ teaspoon garlic powder
¼ teaspoon cumin or curry
    powder (optional)
1-2 tablespoons oil (optional)

Mix the first four ingredients. You may also add cumin for taste and oil for a creamier texture. Refrigerate and use as dressing over cooked vegetables or as a dip.

ALMOND SALAD DRESSING

½ cup skinless almonds
1 clove minced garlic
½ cup olive oil

juice of ½ lemon
½ teaspoon salt

Process all the ingredients in a blender. Store and use as needed over salads.

CREAMED ZUCCHINI

1 zucchini
1 tablespoon olive oil or ¼ ripe
    avocado

chopped fresh dill (optional)
Spike or other seasoning
    to taste

Wash and trim zucchini. Dice into ½-inch pieces and cook in a small amount of water (enough to cover the zucchini) until soft (about 20 minutes). Put half the zucchini (with very little water) into a blender and process with Spike or other seasoning and oil or avocado. Pour mixture into a bowl over the unblended half of the zucchini. Serve cold with dill sprinkled on top.

SPANISH OMELETTE

4 eggs	1 diced tomato
¼ teaspoon garlic powder	½ diced red or green pepper
¼ teaspoon paprika	2 tablespoons olive oil
¼ teaspoon salt	

In a bowl, beat eggs with fork or whisk, adding the three seasonings as you go. Then add the tomato and pepper and pour mixture in a large skillet in which oil has been preheated. Cook slowly over low flame with the lid on.

CORAL DRESSING

1 diced ripe tomato	½ cup olive oil
1 diced half-sour pickle	

Process all the ingredients in a blender. Use on raw vegetables or over asparagus.

NATURAL SWEETS
YUMMY CUSTARD

5 cups unsweetened apple juice	1 teaspoon vanilla
4 tablespoons agar flakes	2 tablespoons carob powder
4 tablespoons tahini	coconut flakes or chopped
4 tablespoons arrowroot powder	pecans

Bring to a boil 4 of the 5 cups apple juice with the agar flakes. Meanwhile, mix in a blender the remaining cup of apple juice, the tahini, and the arrowroot. Add blenderized mixture to boiling mixture and simmer 5 minutes. Add vanilla. For variety, pour half the mixture back into blender, add carob powder, and process. Pour into bowl and let cool. The no-carob half cools separately (take off the stove and set aside). Refrigerate and serve in tall glass goblets, alternating layers of the vanilla and the carob, with a carob swirl on top plus coconut or pecans. Delicious and decorative; a real treat.

INSTANT PAREVE CHEESECAKE

Crust
1½ cups granola
¼ cup sesame oil
1 cup toasted slivered almonds
¾ cup toasted coconut flakes

Filling
2 mashed cakes of firm tofu
1 tablespoon carob powder
1 teaspoon vanilla
¼ teaspoon cinnamon
¾ cup honey
1 tablespoon tahini

Mix together all the ingredients for the crust. Press into a 9-inch pie plate. In a large bowl, mix together all the ingredients for the filling. Fill crust, decorate, chill, and serve.

ROUND HALVAH

½ cup tahini
½ cup finely ground date sugar
    (powdered dates) or ¼ cup
    maple syrup

¼ cup ground almonds
1 teaspoon vanilla
    powdered almonds or
    coconut flakes

Mix all the ingredients together. Mold into balls, roll in powdered almonds or coconut and refrigerate (can be kept in freezer for long-term storage).

NICE CREAM

4 teaspoons raw cashew nuts
4 teaspoons soymilk powder
4 cups unsweetened pineapple
    juice
4 heaping tablespoons frozen
    orange juice concentrate

2 ripe bananas
1 cup crushed pineapple
    or strawberries or peaches

In a blender, process the first three ingredients. Then add orange juice concentrate and reprocess. While blender is running, add fruit. Pour into a container and freeze. Makes 2 quarts.

SNOWBALLS

raisins
apricots (unsulfured)
dates (skinned under warm
    water and then pitted)
figs
currants

prunes (pitted)
ground nuts (filberts, brazils,
    or walnuts) (optional)
coconut flakes or ground
    cashews or almond meal

Put through a food grinder any amount or proportions of the dried fruits. (Add the optional nuts at this time.) Mix well, wet hands, and form 1-inch balls. Roll in coconut, cashews, or almond meal. Store in refrigerator. This is Nature's candy.

NUTTY HEALTH BARS

1 cup toasted oatmeal (pretoast
    in oven)
¼ cup ground sesame seeds
1 cup nut pieces (any kind
    except peanuts)

½ cup raw honey
¼ cup carob powder

Mix the first four ingredients together. Roll out on wax paper, sprinkle with carob powder, and shape into a roll. Refrigerate to harden (wrapped in the wax paper). Slice as needed.

RAW CAKE

1 cup filberts (or any other nut)
½ cup apricots, prunes, or other
    dried fruit
¾ cup honey

1 cup coconut flakes
1 cup wheat germ
¼ teaspoon anise or rum
    or almond extract

Put nuts and dried fruit through a food grinder. Add remaining ingredients, mix, and form into a roll. Wrap in wax paper and refrigerate. Slice as needed.

TOFU PIE

1 cup sunflower seeds, walnuts,
  and sesame seeds in any
  proportion
1½ cakes cubed firm tofu
  (bean curd)
½ cup maple syrup

2 eggs
  juice of ½ lemon
1 teaspoon vanilla
1 peeled, diced apple
2 tablespoons of wheat germ

Grind seeds and nuts in a nut mill. Then press into oiled
pie pan to create a "shell." Process the remaining ingredients in
a blender, adding the wheat germ only if the mixture is too
liquid. Pour blended mixture into pie shell and bake 1 hour
at 350°F.

VARIATION: Add whole blueberries to mixture (after pouring
  into shell) and sprinkle shredded coconut on top.

E-Z APPLE PIE

4 peeled, cored, and diced apples
2 beaten eggs
2 teaspoons vanilla
½ cup maple syrup

⅓ cup water
¾ cup whole wheat flour
¾ cup ground walnuts
2 teaspoons cinnamon (optional)

Mix all the ingredients together. Put into a 9-inch oiled pie
plate and bake for 45 minutes at 350°F.

E-Z PEACH PIE

4 cups peeled and diced peaches
1 cup maple syrup
2 beaten eggs
½ cup sesame or other oil
2 teaspoons vanilla
2 cups whole wheat flour

2 teaspoons baking soda
2 teaspoons Jamaica rum
  (optional)
1 cup presoaked raisins
1 cup chopped walnuts

Mix all the ingredients together. Pour into oiled pie plate and
bake for 45 minutes at 350°F.

C. FESTIVE MEALS

Whether it's for the Sabbath or a holiday, for entertaining guests, or even when you want to treat yourself and your family to a special gourmet meal, there is no limit to the creativity that you can express with foods, without deviating drastically from good nutritional principles. Following are some of my favorite recipes; most of them are printed here for the first time. Enjoy!

SOUPS

MINA'S POTATO SOUP

6 cups water
1 diced potato
1 grated potato
1 grated carrot
1 chopped celery stalk

handful of fresh or dried
    mushrooms
¼ teaspoon caraway seeds
salt
pepper

Combine all ingredients and cook until soft.

COOL SUMMER SOUP

2 large cucumbers
salt
2 cups protein broth (from
    Dr. Bronner's Protein
    Seasoning)
2 cups plain yogurt
1 tablespoon olive oil

1-2 cloves finely minced garlic
2 tablespoons finely chopped
    walnuts
2 tablespoons chopped chives
    or scallion greens
fresh mint

Peel and thinly slice cucumbers. Sprinkle with salt and let stand 20-30 minutes. Prepare protein broth ahead of time and let cool. Mix into yogurt and slowly beat in oil (use hand beater). Rinse cucumber slices and add to yogurt mixture. Add garlic, walnuts and chives and mix well. Refrigerate before serving. Garnish with fresh mint.

ICEBERG SOUP

1 head of iceberg lettuce
1 large ripe tomato
1 carrot
1 tablespoon olive oil
1 diced onion

1 cup diced mushrooms
1 finely chopped celery stalk
½ grated carrot (optional)
Spike or onion and garlic
powders or other seasonings

Sauté onion and mushrooms together; set aside. Take off a few leaves from a head of iceberg lettuce, slice into noodle shapes, and put aside. Cut the rest of the lettuce into chunks. Put the tomato (cut into chunks) in the blender first and then the lettuce. Use the carrot as a "pusher" and blenderize. Add seasoning. Before serving, mix in the lettuce "noodles," sautéd onions and mushrooms, celery, and grated carrot (if desired). Serve cold.

EXODUS KNEIDLACH

(Especially good for Passover)

12 whole wheat matzos
2 finely chopped onions
8 tablespoons olive oil
2 beaten eggs

1 cup warm water
1 teaspoon garlic powder
1 teaspoon salt
finely chopped parsley

Break the matzos by hand and process in blender into matzoh meal (make sure blender container is absolutely dry). Sauté onions in half the oil, until transparent, and then set aside. In a separate bowl, beat the eggs with a fork, add the rest of the oil and the warm water. Mix well. Add the garlic powder, salt, and parsley leaves. Mix. Add as much matzoh meal as will be absorbed by the liquid to create a soft dough consistency. Refrigerate for 2 hours. Then form 1-inch balls (wet your palms first) and put them into boiling water or soup. Cook 30 minutes or longer.

SALADS

STUFFED CELERY

celery stalks
Filling
1 tofu cake (½ pound)

juice of ½ lemon
1 diced dill pickle
1 tablespoon cider vinegar

Process all the filling ingredients in a blender, then stuff the celery stalks.

ISRAELI SALAD

1 ripe finely diced tomato
½ chopped green pepper
1 peeled and diced cucumber
2 chopped scallions

2 tablespoons olive oil
2 teaspoons fresh lemon juice
¼ teaspoon salt

Mix in a cup oil, lemon juice, and salt. Pour over vegetables, toss, and marinate for 30 minutes before serving.

RAINBOW SALAD

carrots, finely grated
raw beets, finely grated

shredded green cabbage

Place equal amounts of carrots, beets, and cabbage in separate bowls. Add a different dressing to each bowl and rearrange in an attractive display on a large serving platter.

Suggested dressings: For the cabbage, Cucumber Dressing (to follow); for the carrots, Pineapple-Raisin Dressing (to follow); for the beets, apple juice.

Cucumber Dressing

½ cup peeled, grated cucumber
½ cup plain yogurt
1 tablespoon cider vinegar
1 tablespoon honey
¼ teaspoon salt (optional)

1 teaspoon kelp (optional)
1 mashed, hard-boiled egg
1 teaspoon minced onion
1 teaspoon fresh, finely minced
    marjoram (presoak if dry)

Put the ingredients in a glass jar, cover, and shake. Use over raw vegetables or mix with shredded green cabbage in Rainbow Salad.

Pineapple-Raisin Dressing

½ cup raisins
1 cup water
1 cup pineapple juice
    (unsweetened canned
    or fresh)

½ cup small chunks pineapple
    (optional)

Presoak raisins in water for 24 hours. (If you forgot, do the "instant" method of soaking in hot water for 5 minutes.) Mix with pineapple juice and pour over Rainbow Salad. Mix well. Pineapple chunks are an interesting addition.

Main Dishes

Beetburgers

5 medium beet roots
6 cups water

3 beaten eggs
1 cup wheat germ

Boil beet roots in water until semisoft. Pour off the water draining beets well. Rub the beets under running water to remove the peel. Grate the roots and add the eggs and as much plain wheat germ as it takes to get a good consistency. Form patties and bake in moderate oven for 20 minutes on one side and then turn over for another 15 minutes. Serve plain or with sauce. This recipe is delicious, nutritious, and free of salt or seasoning.

VEGGIE CASSEROLE

1 broccoli	½ teaspoon paprika
1 cauliflower	½ teaspoon salt
3 beaten eggs	½ teaspoon curry powder
½ teaspoon garlic powder	

Wash broccoli and cauliflower and break into flowerets. Cook or steam for 5 to 6 minutes until semisoft. To the eggs, add the garlic powder, paprika, salt, and curry powder and beat again. Mix eggs and vegetables and put into oiled pan and bake for 15 to 20 minutes in a moderate oven.

ALMOND ROAST

1 cup ground almonds	1 finely chopped green pepper
2 tablespoons vegetable oil	1 teaspoon minced parsley
1 teaspoon finely chopped onion	seasoning to taste (Spike or
2 cups cooked red beans	other)
2 cups whole wheat bread crumbs	

Mix all the ingredients together and shape into a loaf. Bake for 30 minutes in a moderate oven. Slice after it cools slightly. Top with Pareve Gravy or Onion Sauce (recipes below).

PAREVE GRAVY

4 cups water
1 cup cashews
1 onion cut in chunks
¼ teaspoon salt
½ teaspoon miso (fermented
    soybean paste)

½ teaspoon soy sauce
1 cup chopped mushrooms
    (optional
1 tablespoon sesame oil
    (optional)

Process in a blender the water, cashews, and onion. Put this mixture in a saucepan and bring to a boil, stirring until thick. Turn off heat and add salt, miso and soy sauce to taste. If you decide to add mushrooms, sauté them in the oil and then chop fine. Serve over vegetarian roasts, nutburgers, etc.

ONION SAUCE

2 tablespoons finely chopped
    onion
2 tablespoons butter
1 tablespoon rice polish
    or whole wheat flour

1½ cups water (either tap or leftover
    from vegetable cooking)
2 teaspoons soy sauce
½ teaspoon salt
    dash pepper (optional)

Sauté onion in butter until light brown. Stir in rice polish or flour and keep stirring until golden color. Pour in water, soy sauce, salt, and pepper. Cook and stir until thickened.

JAPANESE SPREAD

2 tablespoons sesame oil
1 large grated carrot
2 chopped onions

1 teaspoon soy sauce
3 teaspoons plain tahini

Sauté the carrot and onion in oil. When golden, add soy sauce and plain tahini. Mix and serve on rice cakes as a special treat.

VEGETARIAN CHOPPED LIVER II

5 chopped medium onions
  tablespoon oil
½ pound brown lentils (cooked
    until soft)

5 hard-boiled eggs
½ cup walnuts (or other nuts)
½ teaspoon Spike or other
    natural seasoning

Sauté onions in oil. Combine all the ingredients and pass through a food grinder. Mix with favorite seasoning. Chill and serve scoops on a bed of lettuce, decorated with tomato slices and stuffed olives.

SHISH KEBAB

baked potatoes
steamed yellow squash
cauliflower
roasted green peppers
cooked carrots

cooked celery (destring before
    cooking by breaking in half
    and peeling strings)
broccoli
falafel ball (optional)

Cut all ingredients into bite size cubes. String on a wooden or stainless steel skewer any combination of chunks of the ingredients. Roast a few minutes in the oven after wetting with your favorite curry sauce, and serve over brown rice, which is on a bed of lettuce. Have more curry sauce on the table for the rice.

GEFILTE DISH

2 cakes tofu
2 good-sized parsley roots
    (not parsnip)
2 stalks celery
2 large onions
¾ cup ground sunflower seeds
    (raw) (or cashew nuts)
3 tablespoons wheat germ

2 beaten eggs
1 teaspoon salt
1 teaspoon honey
Garnish
2 sliced onions
2 stalks celery (cut in sticks)
2 diagonally sliced carrots

Put the tofu, parsley, celery, and onion through a food grinder. Add the remaining ingredients and mix. Put into a clean white cotton cloth (at least 15 inches × 15 inches), form into roll, twist into slight crescent (so it can fit into pot) and then roll up the cotton around it. (For extra security, you may want to put a few stitches with white thread to hold the flap.) Put into a large (wide) stainless steel pot, adding enough salt water to cover the roll, add the garnish, and cook together for about 45 minutes. Lift out the roll onto a flat plate (by lifting up from the bottom with a spatula on one side and supporting the cotton with your hand on the other side, after it has cooled enough). Let cool to room temperature and then refrigerate. Place the sliced carrots and the sticks of celery and some of the liquid in a separate bowl. After 2 hours, or even the next day uncover the roll carefully. Make diagonal ¾-inch slices with a wide knife or spatula. Place each piece on a plate with a lettuce leaf and decorate with 2 sices of carrot on top. Serve with prepared red horseradish. If the "fish" is dry you can pour a bit of its cooking liquid over it. This is a perfect Shabbat appetizer, to be served cold. Prepare on Friday.

CHOLENT

1 part red kidney beans	1 or 2 sliced carrots
1 part chick peas	1 chopped onion
½ part large white lima beans	1 or 2 chopped celery stalks
½ part barley	*Seasoning:* (If 1 part = 1 cup, use
½ part mung beans	½ teaspoon of each spice.)
2 potatoes (in chunks)	Spike, miso, paprika, cumin

Soak the beans, peas, and barley overnight in enough water to cover. Next morning, cook 1 hour. Then add potatoes, carrots, onion, celery, and lots of seasonings. Mix and cook for 1 more hour. Add a bit of sesame oil, cover and put into 250°F oven for a few hours.

FESTIVE FRUIT PLATTER

Possible color scheme
   Yellow (peaches)
   Black (prunes)
   Yellow (pineapple)
   Red (cherries)
   Orange (apricots)
   Green (honeydew)

Orange (cantaloupe)
White (pears)
Black (raisins)
White (peeled apple slices)
Red (watermelon)
Blue (blueberries)

For a festive fruit meal, organize a multicolored plate of a wide variety of fresh or dried (presoaked, unsulfured) fruits, arranged with contrasting colors and shapes (chunks, balls, sliced, etc.) adjacent to each other to create eye appeal. Use the top of a fresh pineapple (cut across at least ½ inch below the stem to create a base) as a decorative centerpiece. Have on hand pitchers of two kinds of dressing: *cashew cream* (blenderize cashew nuts, apple juice plus some dates with their skins rubbed off under warm water and then pitted) and *bananaberry cream* (ripe bananas put through a juicer followed by some red strawberries).

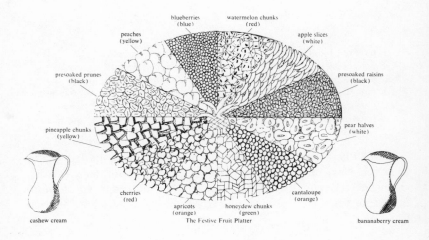

blueberries (blue)　　watermelon chunks (red)

peaches (yellow)　　　　　　　　　　apple slices (white)

presoaked prunes (black)　　　　　　　　presoaked raisins (black)

pineapple chunks (yellow)　　　　　　　　pear halves (white)

cherries (red)　　　　　　　　　cantaloupe (orange)

apricots (orange)　honeydew chunks (green)

cashew cream　　　　The Festive Fruit Platter　　　　bananaberry cream

9

Jewish Vegetarian Groups
and Activities

A. INTERNATIONAL GROUPS

The international center for Jewish vegetarian activities is the Jewish Vegetarian Society. Its headquarters is at *Bet Teva,* 855 Finchley Road, London, N. W. 11 (telephone 01-455-0692). The society has been printing a quarterly publication, the *Jewish Vegetarian,* since September 1966. Generally, each issue includes an editorial, articles relating Judaism and vegetarianism, a column about vegetarianism in Israel, announcements of society and related events, book reviews, recipes, and news about the society and its members. Its editor, Philip Pick, has edited *The Tree of Life,* a collection of articles and editorials which appeared in the magazine (see bibliography).

The Jewish Vegetarian Society sponsors many events and activities related to its goals. Its motto, which appears on the masthead of the *Jewish Vegetarian,* comes from Isaiah's prophecy about the future ideal age: ". . . they shall not hurt nor destroy in all My holy mountain." It has branches in many parts of the world and is currently establishing a branch in Jerusalem, its spiritual center. The society publishes and distributes many articles showing the relationship between Judaism and vegetarianism. There are two types of membership available: one for practicing vegetarians, who do not eat flesh foods, and another

111

for nonvegetarians who are in sympathy with the movement. The origins of the society shows how one person, one letter, one simple act can have a great influence. Philip Pick's daughter, Vivien, wrote a letter about vegetarianism to the *London Jewish Chronicle* in 1965, in which she asked people interested in joining a Jewish vegetarian group to contact her. The response was great, and the result was the Jewish Vegetarian Society.[1]

From its inception in 1966, Philip L. Pick has been the editor of the *Jewish Vegetarian*. He was president of the society for many years and was recently made an honorary life president. He has written many powerful editorials and articles and has spoken at conferences all over the world on the society's goals. He wrote:

> Shall we participate in the use of poisoned carcasses of birds and beasts for food, and ask for a perfect healing? Above all, shall we harden our hearts to the cries of tormented creatures reared in the captivity and darkness of factory farms, and ask for pity and compassion for ourselves and our infants?
>
> Love of humanity, peace, sustenance, and good health, the common birthright of all peoples, cannot be achieved on the basis of the desire for flesh.[2]

The present president of the Jewish Vegetarian Society is Stanley Rubens. He has also been very active in promoting the society's goals through articles, speeches, and administrative work. His strong feelings toward vegetarianism are indicated in the following selections:

> I believe man's downfall is paralleled by his cruelty to animals. In creating slaughterhouses for them he has created slaughterhouses for himself. . . . What is the future for mankind? When the Day of Judgment comes, we will be given that same justice that we gave to the less fortunate fellow creatures who have been in our power.[3]
>
> It is not only possible, but essential for an orthodox Jew to be vegetarian.[4]

B. NATIONAL GROUPS

There is an active North American Jewish Vegetarian Society, which is affiliated with the international Jewish Vegetarian Society. It has about 1,200 members and is led by Jonathan Wolf, who holds many Jewish vegetarian events in his home. He is a committed, orthodox Jew, who believes that all the reasons for becoming vegetarian have roots in Jewish values.

Mr. Wolf teaches a unique course, "Judaism and Vegetarianism" at the Lincoln Square Synagogue in New York. In this course he examines vegetarian values in Jewish sources, compassion for animals, feeding the hungry, ecology, *bal tashchit* ("thou shalt not waste"), and preservation of health. He utilizes material from the Torah and other Jewish sources, modern *responsa,* Jewish legal codes, writings of Rabbi Kook, Joseph Albo, and other Jewish scholars, and fiction by vegetarian authors such as Isaac Bashevis Singer.

The group frequently celebrates the sabbath and Jewish holidays at Jonathan Wolf's home. He recently had about 50 guests for a vegetarian seder. He has been extremely creative in relating vegetarian values to the holidays. Especially interesting is the annual vegetarian *Tu Bishvat* seder, conducted in the tradition of the Kabbalists of Safed (not vegetarians). The seder is conducted with a tasting of samples of the seven species of grains and fruits mentioned in the Bible, accompanied with related readings from the Bible, Talmud, Prophets, and other holy writings, with four special cups of wine.[5] There is much singing, merriment, good feeling, warmth, community, games, and blessings of thanks.

The group prints a newsletter, *The Sprout,* to keep members and interested persons informed about local news and activities. They also produce, reprint, and distribute literature relating Judaism and vegetarianism. Additional plans of Mr. Wolf and the group include organizing a kosher natural food co-op, producing a kosher vegetarian guide and cookbook, translating

Rabbi Kook's vegetarian writings, and creating more materials on all aspects of Jewish vege₍arianism.

An article about Jonathan Wolf and other American Jewish vegetarians appeared in the *National Jewish Monthly* in April 1976.[6] The article states that there is evidence that the percentage of U. S. Jewish vegetarians is increasing; there has been an increase in interest in vegetarianism at northeastern colleges with large Jewish population; Camp Ramah, a Jewish camp in Plamer, Massachusetts, has provided a special diet for vegetarians; Jews become vegetarians for a variety of reasons—some are committed *halachic* (Jewish law) vegetarians, but for others, Jewish sources are incidental to their commitment to vegetarianism.

Recently, Alex Harris has been trying to bring American Jewish vegetarians together in a dues-paying organization that would provide literature and information about Jewish vegetarian activities to its members. For information, write Alex Harris, c/o American Jewish Vegetarian Society, P.O. Box 403591, Miami Beach, Florida 33140. An article about Alex's vegetarian projects recently appeared in the *Miami Beach Citizen News.*

There is a vegetarian hotel in Woodridge, New York (the Catskills). It was founded in 1920 by its present owner, Fannie Shaffer. It provides a wide variety of kosher food and has lectures and other activities related to vegetarianism, nutrition, and health. Information and directions can be obtained by writing the Vegetarian Hotel at P. O. Box 457, Woodridge, N. Y. 12789 (phone: 914-434-4455).

Louis Berman, professor of psychology and staff counselor at the Student Counseling Service, University of Illinois, Chicago Circle, has written a book, *Vegetarianism and Jewish Tradition,* which will be published by Ktav in New York. Professor Berman has lectured on vegetarianism in Chicago, Denver, Los Angeles, and Dayton, Ohio, and has taught an evening adult education class in vegetarian cooking in his home town of Evanston, Illinois.

Izak Luchinsky has been very active in organizing various vegetarian programs in the Baltimore, Maryland, area. An article about his vegetarian activities appeared in the *Baltimore Jewish Times.*

C. VEGETARIANISM IN ISRAEL

In Israel today, vegetarianism is an active movement. There are two organizations, the Israel Vegetarian Union and the Haifa Vegetarian Society.[7] It has been estimated that there are about 80,000 vegetarians in Israel.[8] Generally, there is a column in each issue of the *Jewish Vegetarian* on vegetarianism in Israel.

Amirim is a completely vegetarian community in Israel.[9] It is the only vegetarian-naturalist village without livestock in the world. It is presently the home of about 60 vegetarian and naturalist families. It is located in the Galilee, near the city of Safed. Its elevation of 600 meters above the Mediterranean Sea and 800 meters above the Sea of Galilee is such that both can be seen from the village. Many families in Amirim provide lodging and meals to vacationers; several have natural foods kitchens and others are vegetarian. Vacationers can eat at a variety of homes to sample different types of meals and meet a variety of people. The village store contains a full range of organic foods but no meat, fish, or cigarettes. There is a pool and other recreational facilities available for vacationers.

The Ashkenazi chief rabbi of Israel, Rabbi Shlomo Goren, the chief rabbi of the Haifa district, Rabbi Shear Yashuv Cohen, and Rabbi Cohen's father, Rabbi David Cohen (the Nazir) are all vegetarians (see biographies in Chapter 10 for more information about them). These were the first three rabbis to reach the Western Wall after the 1967 war.[10] There have been three vegetarian chief rabbis since the establishment of Israel in 1948.[11]

Mordecai Ben-Porat, a member of the Rabin (Labour Party) government in Israel, has introduced a bill in the Knesset (Israeli parliament) that would outlaw flesh eating in Israel.[12] He contends that Israel's hard-pressed economy cannot bear the massive National Health Service costs related to diseases due to the eating of flesh foods. The bill was sent to a special committee for investigation but died when the Labour Party lost the election.

Mr. Ben-Porat also called for a National Obesity Treatment Institute and a halt to the import of beef and other foods rich in animal fat.[13] He claims that an improvement in Israeli eating habits could save 4.266 billion Israeli pounds and $150 million in foreign currency for food imports.

Replying, then Health Minister Victor Shemtov said that studies have verified that bad eating habits cause "cruel and cumulative clinical effects" in persons between the ages of 40 and 50.[14] In 1975, nearly 7,000 Israelis died of heart disease and diabetes (this constituted 30% of all adult deaths that year) and both diseases, Shemtov states, are "closely associated with faulty food intake and selection."[15]

Mitzpe Hayamim is a health center run on the basis of vegetarian diet and homeopathic medical treatment. It has an excellent location on a hill 600 meters above sea level overlooking the Sea of Galilee and the plain of the Jordan Valley. In its serene surroundings and pure mountain air, patients find peace, tranquility, relaxation, and a chance to meditate.[16]

Tel Aviv University's Medical School has established a foundation to conduct research into nature cures. The foundation also strives to guide and increase knowledge of natural health and to undertake research into nutrition, health, and various branches of natural therapy. The foundation has been endowed by a grant of £250,000 by Dr. and Mrs. Moshe Ishai.

As previously mentioned, Philip Pick has been active in setting up a Jewish Vegetarian Society branch in Israel.[17] It held its first public meeting at the Hebrew Union College in Jerusalem in March 1981. About 150 enthusiastic people attended and heard talks from Mr. Pick, retired Justice of the Supreme Court Zvi Berenson, Dan Barel, chairman of the Israel branch, and Albert Kaplan, a Jerusalem organizer. Jonah Goren described a 40-bedroom vegetarian farm and holiday center being constructed in Ashkelon, Israel. He is also providing premises for a nature cure college, and the Jewish Vegetarian Society is assisting in this project.[18]

The Summer 1980 issue of the *Jewish Vegetarian* reported details of initial plans for the Israeli branch of the Jewish Vegetarian Society:

(1) It is proposed that a freehold property in Rahavia, Jerusalem, be purchased.

(2) This would comprise a meeting hall, office, and library for the further promotion in Israel of the Jewish Vegetarian Society's aims.

(3) These facilities would be available to the Israel Vegetarian Union and as an office for the Middle East Region of the International Vegetarian Union.

(4) Rooms fitted with all facilities would be available for permanent or temporary accommodation, preferably, but not exclusively, for retired persons.

(5) The premises could be used for a naturopathic center, for both practice and study.

The International Jewish Vegetarian Society is trying to raise funds to help make this dream a reality.

Vegetarianism has recently started flourishing in Jerusalem, with several health-food shops, two new publications, and vegetarian restaurants sprouting up recently. The health-food stores include "Hameshek," which also has a vegetarian restaurant, "A Bit of the Garden of Eden," in the German Colony, and the "Hadassah Health Food Store" on Jaffa Road.[19]

Panina Tal publishes in Hebrew a new magazine called *Natural Health,* which is dedicated to preventive medicine and natural cure. She has a master's degree in biology and is a resident of Jerusalem.[20] A publication, *New Age,* gives vegetarian-oriented information in both Hebrew and English. Its address is P.O. Box 2259, Jerusalem. Both publications are trying to raise funds in order to expand.[21]

Yisrael Meir Kaplan, Jerusalem, is trying to set up a vegan settlement. He has held meetings in three main cities and welcomes both novices and experts in various fields to contact him.[22]

Hal and Shelly Cohen have established the Orr Shalom Vegetarian Children's Home at 48 Beit Zayit Street, D.N. Harei Yehuda.[23] It is affiliated with the international Jewish Vegetarian Society. The Cohens hope that "Orr Shalom" will become a center for spreading vegetarian ideas and ideals throughout Israel.

10

Biographies of Famous Jewish Vegetarians

In this chapter brief biographies will be given of famous Jews who were vegetarians for all or part of their lives.[1] The author would appreciate hearing about other Jewish vegetarians who have not been included and/or significant facts that have been omitted from these biographies.

AGNON, SHMUEL YOSEF (1888-1970)

Shmuel Yosef Agnon is a central figure in modern Hebrew fiction. He wrote many novels and short stories about major contemporary spiritual concerns. He won the Israel Prize for Literature in 1954 and 1958 and the Nobel Prize in Literature in 1966, the first time that this honor was given to a Hebrew writer. His folk epic, *The Bridal Canopy,* was widely recognized as one of the cornerstones of modern Hebrew literature.

Agnon was a devout Jew who spent much of his life in Israel. He was extremely devoted to vegetarianism. He wove vegetarian themes into many of his stories, as in the following excerpt:

> He received the Sabbath with sweet song and chanted the hallowing tunefully over raisin wine. . . . The table was well

spread with all manner of fruit, beans, greenstuffs and good
pies, . . . but of flesh and fish there was never a sign. . . .
The old man and his wife had never tasted flesh since
reaching maturity.[2]

Agnon's great sensitivity to all creatures can be seen in the
following excerpt from his speech upon receiving the Nobel Prize
for Literature:

Lest I slight any creature, I must also mention the domestic
animals, the beasts and the birds from whom I have learned.
Job said long ago (35:11): "Who teacheth us more than the
beasts of the earth, and maketh us wiser than the fowls of
heaven?" Some of what I have learned from them I have
written in my books, but I fear that I have not learned as
much as I should have done, for when I hear a dog bark,
or a bird twitter, or a cock crow, I do not know whether
they are thanking me for all I have told of them or calling
me to account.[3]

COHEN, RABBI DAVID (THE NAZIR)

Rabbi Cohen made a major contribution to Jewish vegetarianism by collecting and editing the Jewish vegetarian ideas of Rabbi
Kook.[4] He was known as the "Nazir of Jerusalem" because he
adopted all the obligations of the Nazarite as described in the
Torah; he did not drink wine or cut his hair for a specific period.

He is the father of the present chief rabbi of Haifa, Rabbi
Shear Yashuv Cohen, and of the wife of the Ashkenazi chief rabbi
of Israel, Rabbi Goren.

COHEN, RABBI SHEAR YASHUV[5]

Rabbi Shear Yashuv Cohen has been a vegetarian from birth
and is a patron of the Jewish Vegetarian Society. He was graduated
in 1947 from Rabbi Kook's Universal Yeshiva in Jerusalem and
was ordained a rabbi by the late Ashkenazi Chief Rabbi Harzog.
From 1948 to 1953, he was chaplain in the Israeli Defense Forces

and chief chaplain of the Israeli Air Forces (1952-53). His many positions include dean of the Harvey Fischel Institute for Research in Jewish Law and Seminary for Rabbis and Rabbinical Judges; member of the City Council of Jerusalem (from 1955); deputy mayor of Jerusalem (1965-75); and chief rabbi of Haifa (since 1975).

GORDON, AARON DAVID (1856-1922)

Aaron David Gordon was a Hebrew writer who wrote numerous articles on labor, Zionism, and the Jewish destiny. As a strong advocate of the kibbutz (collective settlement) approach, his writings influenced the Jewish Labor Movement throughout the world. He hoped that kibbutzim would be vegetarian settlements, dependent on the land for their produce.

Gordon believed that Zionism would obtain self-fulfillment through working the land. He came to Israel at the age of 48 and spent many years farming. He saw the state of Israel as a challenge to Jews to make a contribution to humanity. He believed that the Jews would be tested through their attitudes and behavior toward the Arabs.

The importance that Gordon placed on vegetarianism can be seen in the following selection:

> The attitude toward vegetarianism . . . the attitude toward living creatures is . . . the clearest test of our attitude towards life and towards the world as it really is. . . . The ethical regard toward living creatures that involves no hope of reward, no utilitarian motive—secret or open, such as honor, shows us . . . the significance of righteousness and all the other desired traits . . . righteousness, truth, and the like— and eating living creatures!"[6]

GOREN, RABBI SHLOMO (1917-   )

Rabbi Shlomo Goren has been the Ashkenazic chief rabbi of Israel from 1972. He was formerly the Ashkenazic chief rabbi of Tel Aviv-Jaffa and the chief rabbi of the Israeli Defense Forces. In that capacity, he was the first to conduct a service at the liberated Western Wall in 1967.

Rabbi Goren has given many *responsa* on issues related to modern technology and conditions of modern warfare. He has published a collection of essays on the festivals and holy days. His comprehensive commentary on the section *Berakhot* of the Jerusalem Talmud won the Israel Prize in 1961.

The Rabbi's wife is a life-long vegetarian, having been reared in an orthodox vegetarian home in Jerusalem.[7]

KACYZNE, ALTER (1885-1941)

Alter Kacyzne was born in Lithuania but spent most of his creative years in Warsaw, where many of his plays were successfully staged. His works include many dramatic poems, ballads, short stories, and one full-length novel, *The Strong and the Weak,* which won much praise for its great historical-political significance. His writing often dealt with people's inhumanity.

Kacyzne became a vegetarian at the age of 18, after a curious dream in which he was forced to eat a roasted child. His vegetarian beliefs were well known in Poland. He and his wife hosted well-attended vegetarian receptions. He was beaten to death with sticks and clubs by Nazis in the Ukraine in 1941 and was buried in a mass grave.[8]

KAFKA, FRANZ (1883-1924)

Franz Kafka was a Czech-born, German novelist whose writing had tremendous influence on western literature and art. His many books include *The Castle, The Trial,* and *The Great Wall of China.* His novels have been translated into many languages, including Hebrew, and have been adapted for movies, plays, and operas. The action in his books generally centers around the hero's search for identity.

Kafka was attracted to vegetarianism for health and ethical

reasons. While viewing fish at an aquarium, he said, "Now I can look at you in peace; I don't eat you any more." He had little faith in conventional doctors; he was interested in the benefits of nature-cure and raw-foods diets. He was also involved in anti-vivisection activities.[9]

KOOK (SOMETIMES SPELLED KUK), RABBI ABRAHAM ISAAC (1865-1935)

Rabbi Abraham Isaac Kook was the first Ashkenazi chief rabbi of Palestine after the British mandate. He was a very prolific writer who helped inspire many people to move toward spiritual paths. He urged religious people to become involved in social questions and efforts to improve the world.

Among Rabbi Kook's many significant writings is "A Vision of Vegetarianism and Peace," in which he gave his philosophy of vegetarianism. As indicated previously, he believed strongly that God wants people to be vegetarian and that meat was permitted as a concession to people's weakness. He thought that the many prohibitions related to the slaughtering and eating of meat were meant as a scolding and reminder that people should have reverence for life; this would eventually bring people back to vegetarianism in the days of the Messiah.[10]

LEFTWICH, JOSEPH (1892-   )

Joseph Leftwich has been an author, editor, and anthologist. He is considered an authority on Jewish and Yiddish literature. He translated works by Sholom Asch, Max Brod, I. L. Peretz, Zalman Schneur, and Stefan Zweig. He also edited several influential anthologies: *Yisroel, The First Jewish Omnibus* (1933, rev. 1963), a wide selection of Jewish literature from many countries; the *Golden Peacock* (1939), translations for Yiddish poetry; and *The Way We Think* (2 vols., 1969), Yiddish essays in English translation.

Leftwich is an active vegetarian and a patron of the Jewish Vegetarian Society. He has written brief biographies of vegetarian writers, which appeared in the *Jewish Vegetarian,*[11] and an introduction to *The Tree of Life,* a collection of essays relating Judaism and vegetarianism.

MACCOBY, CHAIM ZUNDEL (THE KAMENISTER MAGGID)[12]

The Reverend Chaim Zundel Maccoby was born in Kamenits, Russia. He settled in London in 1890 and preached Torah and vegetarianism in the streets of that city. He taught people to have compassion for all living creatures and how to remain healthy with little money. He was known by many as a great and saintly preacher. He was a dedicated vegetarian who wore cloth shoes all year long to show his abhorrence of leather.

PERETZ, ISAAC LEIB (1852-1915)

I. L. Peretz was a prolific and versatile writer of Hebrew and Yiddish stories and poems. He was one of the founders of modern Yiddish literature as well as an important figure in Hebrew literature. He had many original ideas and used his rich imagination to champion the cause of the oppressed and common people. His compassion and sensitivity encouraged many aspiring authors. He wrote much about the lives of the chasidim, and the Jewish socialist movement was greatly influenced by his ideas.

RAVITCH, MELECH (1893-1976)[13]

Melech Ravitch was considered the dean of Yiddish poetry. His poems occupy nearly a dozen pages in the Yiddish poetry anthology, *The Golden Peacock* (edited by Joseph Leftwich). He compiled an 850-page anthology of material about Jewish Warsaw called the *Warsaw That Was* and wrote about 200 short portrait sketches of Yiddish writers.

Ravitch's poems and essays expressed universal values. He

was a vegetarian most of his life and a patron of the Jewish Vegetarian Society.

ROSEN, RABBI DAVID[14]

Rabbi Rosen is the chief rabbi of Ireland. He received his rabbinic ordination from the Rosh Yeshivah of Ponivez and from Av Bet Din Rabbi Levin. He served as senior minister at the Green and Sea Point Hebrew Congregation in Cape Town, the largest congregation in South Africa; while there, he opposed the inequities in South Africa.

He, his wife, and two young daughters are ethical vegetarians, which they find completely compatible with orthodox Judaism. Rabbi Rosen feels that vegetarianism is growing among Jews in both South Africa and Ireland, and he is a patron of the Jewish Vegetarian Society.

SINGER, ISAAC BASHEVIS (1904-   )

I. B. Singer was born in Poland but came to the United States in 1935. He has been a writer for the New York Yiddish *Daily Forward* under the pen name of Isaac Warshavsky. His best-selling novels include *The Family Moskat, Satan in Goray, The Magician of Lublin, Gimpel the Fool, The Spinoza of Market Street,* and *The Slave.* He won the Nobel Prize for Literature in 1978.

He has been a vegetarian for nearly half a century, primarily because of compassion for animals, and is a patron of the Jewish Vegetarian Society. He received an award from the Vegetarian Information Service in July 1979 for his contributions to literature and vegetarianism.

The following selection is from Singer's novel, *The Estate:*

Zadok had begun to worry about another matter: the eating of meat. How could one be opposed to violence and at the same time consume the flesh of innocent beasts and fowl?

Could there be a justification for this? It was simply a matter of power. Whoever held the knife slaughtered. But he, after all, was against the rule of might. He had already informed Hannah that he would no longer eat meat, but Hannah had answered him with a lament. . . . She wept, complained, and made such a fuss that Zakok give in to her. He would eat meat, if only she would keep still! But the meat didn't agree with him. Hannah bought giblets, heads, feet, entrails, livers. He felt that he was actually swallowing blood and marrow. It would have been possible to kill him, and cook him, in exactly the same way. How can those who torture creatures talk of justice?[15]

The next excerpt is from his short story, "The Slaughterer":

Barely three months had passed since Yoineh Meir had become a slaughterer, but the time seemed to stretch endlessly. He felt as though he were immersed in blood and lymph. His ears were beset by the squawking of hens, the crowing of roosters, the gobbling of geese, the lowing of oxen, the mooing and bleating of calves and goats; wings fluttered, claws tapped on the floor. The bodies refused to know any justification or excuse—every body resisted in its own fashion, tried to escape, and seemed to argue with the Creator to its last breath.

And Yoineh Meir's own mind raged with question. Verily, in order to create the world, the Infinite One had had to shrink His light; there could be no free choice without pain. But since the beasts were not endowed with free choice, why should they have to suffer?[16]

Singer's strong feelings with regard to vegetarianism are indicated in the following selections:

The longer I am a vegetarian, the more I feel how wrong it is to kill animals and eat them. I think that eating meat or fish is a denial of all ideals, even of all religions. How can we pray to God for mercy if we ourselves have no mercy? How can we speak of right and justice if we take an innocent creature and shed its blood? Every kind of killing seems to me savage and I find no justification for it.

I believe that the religion of the future will be based on vegetarianism. As long as people will shed the blood of innocent creatures there can be no peace, no liberty, no harmony between people. Slaughter and justice cannot dwell together.[17]

Early in my life I came to the conclusion that there was no basic difference between man and animals. If a man has the heart to cut the throat of a chicken or a calf, there's no reason he should not be willing to cut the throat of a man.

It took me a long time to come to the decision to be a vegetarian because I was always afraid I'd starve to death. But never did I have a moment in these 15 years when I regretted that decision.[18]

11

Summary

What a glorious religion Judaism is. It mandates compassion, not just for Jews, but for the stranger, even for enemies, and for all of God's creatures. A person without compassion cannot be considered a descendant of Abraham, our father. Jews are to consider the welfare of animals and to avoid *tsa'ar ba'alei chayim,* inflicting pain on any living creature.

Judaism stresses the preservation of life and health. So important is this that to save a life, Jews are commanded to set aside ritual laws related to the Sabbath, *kashrut,* and eating on Yom Kippur.

Judaism places great emphasis on reducing hunger. A Jew who helps to feed a hungry person is considered, in effect, to have fed God. Related to helping the hungry are the important Jewish concepts of pursuing justice, giving charity, showing compassion, and sharing the earth's resources.

Judaism teaches that people are to be co-workers with God in preserving and improving the earth. We are to be stewards and to use God's bounties for the benefit of all. Nothing that has value can be wasted or destroyed unnecessarily.

Judaism emphasizes the need to seek and pursue peace. Great is peace for it is God's name, all God's blessings are contained in it, it must be sought even in times of war, and it will be the first blessing brought by the Messiah.

Vegetarianism is the diet most consistent with these important Jewish ideals: A vegetarian diet does not require the raising of animals in closed, cramped spaces, where they are denied exercise, fresh air, sunlight, and emotional fulfillment. A vegetarian diet is consistent with our body structure and chemistry and is least likely to lead to heart trouble, cancer and other diseases. A vegetarian diet does not require the wasting of grain, land, water, pesticide, fertilizer, and fuel while millions die annually from hunger and its effects. A vegetarian diet is most consistent with the concepts that "the earth is the Lord's," that we are partners with God in preserving and enhancing the world, and we are not to waste or unnecessarily destroy anything of value. A vegetarian diet, by not wasting scarce resources and by not requiring the daily slaughter of helpless creatures of God, is most likely to lead to that day when "nations shall beat their swords into plowshares, their spears into pruning hooks, and not study war any more."

The negative effects of flesh-centered diets are all interconnected: The cruel methods used to raise animals lead to unhealthy animals, which in turn affects human health. The fact that over 80% of all grain grown in the United States is fed to animals contributes to global hunger and energy shortages, both of which lead to greater potential for violence and war; the tremendous amounts of grains grown for animal feed require much fertilizer and pesticides, and their manufacture and use cause extensive air and water pollution. Waters polluted by pesticides, fertilizers, and other chemicals result in fish that are unhealthy to eat. Finally, wars that result from food and energy shortages have extremely harmful effects on animals as well as people. Everything is connected to everything else.

Vegetarianism, by itself, although an important step in the right direction, is not the complete answer to solving problems.

Jews should work to eliminate violations of *tsa'ar ba'alei chayim* related to raising animals for food (until all are vegetarians), scientific testing, the use of animals for furs, and the abuse of animals for sport and entertainment.

Although a vegetarian diet is a positive step for preserving health, Jews should also work for better health through exercise, elimination of junk foods, and other proper hygiene techniques.

Jews should work to see that food saved through vegetarian diets gets to hungry people; they should also strive for better social and economic conditions to enable people in poor countries to grow the food that they need for survival.

In addition to improving the environment through vegetarian diets, Jews should work for better energy, transportation, industrial, and residential systems consistent with the Torah concepts of stewardship and *bal tashchit*.

Finally, consistent with Torah mandates, Jews should in every way seek and pursue peace by working for more equitable sharing of the earth's resources, more harmonious relations among nations, and a reduction of rapidly increasing arms budgets, which take funds from critical human needs such as education, shelter, employment, health, and proper nutrition.

At the close of this book, one final question will be asked of Jews who plan to continue to eat meat: In view of the strong Jewish mandates to be compassionate to animals, preserve health, help feed the hungry, preserve and protect the environment, and seek and pursue peace and the very negative effects flesh-centered diets have in each of these areas, how do you justify not becoming a vegetarian?

Appendix

A. ACTION-CENTERED IDEAS

This book demonstrates that vegetarianism has many positive benefits—for health, the environment, all God's creatures, and the reduction of world hunger. For those who want to do more to help move the world toward vegetarianism, the following suggestions are given:

(1) Become well informed. Learn the facts about vegetarianism from this and other books (see the bibliography). Know how to answer questions on vegetarianism, and use such questions to inform others. Of course, relate to others in a patient and positive way.

(2) Spread the word. Wear a button. Put a bumper sticker on your car. Make up posters. Write timely letters to the editor of your local newspapers. Set up programs and discussions. There are a wide variety of interesting vegetarian slogans on buttons, bumper stickers, and T-shirts. For example:

Happiness is reverence for life. Be vegetarian.

Love animals. Don't eat them.

Why brake for animals if you eat them?

Vegetarianism is good for life.

Use the world vegetarian symbol on correspondence. This will help the vegetarian movement obtain publicity that it badly needs and, because of prohibitive costs, cannot be easily obtained otherwise. Stickers and rubber stamps with the world vegetarian symbol can be obtained from the Jewish Vegetarian Society.

(3) Use the material in this and other vegetarian books in discussions with doctors. Make them aware of the many health benefits of a vegetarian diet.

(4) Ask the rabbi of your synagogue, respectfully, if Jews should eat meat today because of important Jewish principles such as *bal tashchit, tsa'ar ba'alei chayim,* and *pikuach nefesh* that are being violated. Ask if these concepts can be included in sermons and classes.

(5) Request that meat or fish not be served at synagogue and Jewish organizational functions and celebrations, for the reasons presented in this book. Ask school principals and school directors to serve nutritious vegetarian meals.

(6) Ask the rabbi and/or head of a Hebrew school to organize a trip to a slaughterhouse so that people can observe how animals are slaughtered. A trip to a factory farm to see how cattle and chickens are raised would also be very instructive.

(7) Try to arrange a synagogue or organizational session where vegetarian dishes are sampled and recipes exchanged.

(8) Speak or organize an event with a guest speaker on the advantages of vegetarianism and how vegetarianism relates to Judaism.

(9) Get vegetarian books into public and synagogue libraries by donating duplicates, requesting that libraries purchase such books, and, if you can afford it, by buying some and donating them.

(10) Work with others to set up a vegetarian food co-op or restaurant or help support such places if they already exist. Encourage people to patronize such establishments.

(11) Register yourself with a community, library, or school

speakers' bureau. Become informed and start speaking out.

(12) Contact the food editor of your local newspaper and ask that more vegetarian recipes be printed.

(13) When applicable, to raise awareness, indicate how values of the sabbath and festivals are consistent with vegetarian concepts. For example: Point out that the *kiddish* recited before lunch on the sabbath indicates that animals are also to be able to rest on the sabbath day; on *Sukkot,* note that the *sukkah* (temporary dwelling place) is decorated with pictures and replicas of fruits and vegetables (never with animal products); on Yom Kippur, observe the mandate expressed in the prophetic reading of Isaiah to "share thy bread with the hungry," which can be carried out best by not having a diet that wastes much land, grain, water, fuel, and fertilizer.

(14) Support groups that are working to reduce world hunger. Some responsible organizations are:

OXFAM-America, 302 Columbus Avenue, Boston, MA 02116

Care, Inc., Tri-State Regional Office, 660 First Avenue, New York, NY 10016

U.S. Committee for UNICEF, 331 E. 38th Street, New York, NY 10016 (note: not associated with UNESCO; supported by Israel)

Project Relief, P.O. Box 1455, Providence, RI 02901

American Friends Service Committee, 15 Rutherford Place, New York, NY 10003

American Joint Distribution Committee, 60 East 42nd Street, New York, NY 10017 (serves mostly Jews overseas)

These groups generally go beyond merely providing charitable aid to the needy; they strive, in accordance with Maimonides's concept of the highest form of charity, to make people self-reliant in producing their own food.

(15) If people are not willing to become vegetarians, encourage them to at least make a start by giving up at

least red meat and having one or two meatless meals a
week (perhaps Mondays and Thursdays, which were
traditional Jewish fast days).

(16) Do not concentrate only on vegetarianism. It is only
part of the struggle for justice, compassion, and peace.
Become aware and try to affect public policy with
regard to the issues raised in this book: not wasting,
preserving health, showing compassion for animals,
saving human lives, dealing our bread to the hungry,
seeking and pursuing peace.

If you feel that problems of world hunger and of convincing
people to change their diets are so great that your efforts will
have little effect, consider the following:

Our tradition teaches, "It is not thine to complete the task,
but neither art thou free to desist from it."[1] We must make a
start and do whatever we can to improve the world. Judaism
teaches that a person is obligated to protest when there is evil
and to proceed from protest to action (see Question 11, chapter
7). Each person is to imagine that the world is evenly balanced
between the good and the wicked and that his actions can deter-
mine the destiny of the entire world, for good or evil.

Even if little is accomplished, trying to make improvements
will prevent the hardening of your heart and will affirm that you
accept moral responsibility. The very act of consciousness raising
is important because it may lead to future changes.

B. HELPING BRING THE MESSIAH
TO THE WORLD

Judaism teaches that we are heading toward a kingdom of the
Messiah, when "none shall hurt nor destroy in all My holy
mountain" (Isa. 11:19). The Jewish tradition asserts that one
way to speed the coming of the Messiah is to start practicing the
ways that will prevail in the messianic time. For example, the
Talmud teaches that if all Jews properly observed two consecu-

tive sabbaths, the Messiah would immediately come.[2] This means symbolically that when all Jews reach the level when they can fully observe the sabbath in terms of devotion to God and compassion for people and animals, the conditions would be such that the messianic period would have arrived.

According to Rabbi Kook and others, based on the prophecy of Isaiah 11:6-9 (And the wolf shall dwell with the lamb . . ."), the messianic period will be vegetarian. Hence, if all became vegetarian in the proper spirit, with compassion for all animals and human beings, and concern about preserving God's world, perhaps this would mean that the messianic period would be here.

C. THE SERVICE OF THE HEART

Since the destruction of the Temple and end of animal sacrifices, prayer, the service of the heart, has played a major role in Judaism. The following questions related to vegetarianism should be considered as we prepare for prayer:

Can our prayers for compassion be answered when we do not show compassion for God's defenseless creatures? Can our prayers for sustenance be answered when our eating habits deprive many needy people of a portion of God's bounteous harvests? Can our prayers for good health be answered when we consume flesh with high doses of pesticides, antibiotics, and other chemicals. Can our prayers for rain to nourish our crops be answered when so much of that rain is used to grow feedcrops for animals while the hungry pine away for lack of adequate food and water? Can our prayers for peace (*Sim Shalom*)[3] be answered when we do not share God's provisions, thereby perpetuating war and violence? Can we sincerely chant every sabbath morning "All living things shall praise thee . . . (*Nishmas Kol Chai T'vo'rech Et Shim'Choh*)[4] and have a diet that depends on treating some of these living things as machines whose sole purpose is to feed our stomachs?

Are the following words of Isaiah valid today as we fail to show compassion to animals as well as people?

> *I cannot endure iniquity and solemn assembly;*
> *Your new moons and your appointed feasts,*
> *My soul hates.*
> *They have become a burden to me,*
> *That I am weary to bear.*
> *When you spread forth your hands,*
> *I will hide my eyes from you,*
> *Even though you make many prayers,*
> *I will not listen.*
> *Your hands are full of blood.* (Isa 1:12-15)

The following from a poem by Coleridge is also applicable:

> *He prayeth best who loveth best*
> *all things both great and small*
> *For the dear God who loveth us*
> *He made and loveth all.*[5]

The previously told story of Israel Salanter placing compassion for animals ahead of Yom Kippur evening prayers is also relevant.

Rabbi Abraham Joshua Heschel, an outstanding twentieth-century Jewish philosopher, states that more than worship is required by God. "Worship without compassion is worse than self-deception; it is an abomination."[6]

The word "prayer" (*t'filah*) comes from the Hebrew word *l'hit pallel,* which means self-evaluation. Our self-evaluation could be enhanced if we acted with compassion toward hungry people and defenseless creatures.

D.   IMITATION OF GOD

The Jewish tradition asserts that we are to imitate God's actions. This is related to the biblical account of the creation of man in the image of God (Gen. 1:26). Other biblical sources for the commandment to imitate God are found in the statement that we are to be holy as God is holy (Lev. 19:2) and that we are to walk in God's ways (Deut. 10:12).

A rabbinic statement that we should imitate God is that of

Hama bar Hanina in his commentary on the verse, "After the Lord your God ye shall walk" (Deut. 13:5):

> How can man walk after God? Is He not a consuming fire? What is meant is that man ought to walk after (imitate) the attributes of God. Just as the Lord clothes the naked, so you shall clothe the naked. Just as He visits the sick, so you shall visit the sick. Just as the Lord comforted the bereaved, so you shall also comfort the bereaved; just as He buried the dead, so you shall bury the dead.[7]

The rabbis stress that Jews are to imitate God's qualities of kindness, compassion, and forbearance; however, they do not advise that we imitate God in his infrequent attribute of harsh justice.

As the Lord is our shepherd, we are shepherds of voiceless beasts. As God is kind and compassionate to us, we should be considerate of animals.

We should also imitate God in his treatment of animals. He provides vegetation to domestic animals and furnishes food and drink for all beasts of the field. The psalmist declares that "the young lions roar after their prey and seek their food from the Lord" (Ps. 104:21). God provided each animal features it needed for survival. He gave a short tail to animals that feed among the thorns, a long neck to animals that pick high leaves, the ability to endure thirst to the camel, and so forth.

By showing compassion to animals through a vegetarian diet, we help fulfill the commandment to imitate God's ways.

E. OUR WEDDING VOW TO GOD

The Prophet Hosea states that we have, in effect, a wedding vow to God. What are the conditions of our betrothal?

> *I will betroth you unto me forever;*
> *I will betroth you unto me in righteousness*
> *and in justice, in living kindness and in*
> *compassion. I will betroth you unto me in*
> *faithfulness, and you shall know the Lord.* (Hos: 2:21-2)

Orthodox Jews recite these words every weekday morning as they wrap the *tefillin* around their fingers as a symbolic wedding ring.

This wedding vow echoes and reinforces much of what we have said elsewhere in this book. We are wed to God; we are to be co-workers, and the traits that we are to exhibit are righteousness, justice, loving-kindness, and compassion. These important traits, which constitute our wedding vow to God, are echoed in other statements of the prophets:

> *What does the Lord require of you*
> *but that you act justly,*
> *love kindness,*
> *and walk humbly with thy God.* (Mic. 6:8)

> *Thus sayeth the Lord,*
> *"Let not the wise man glory in his wisdom,*
> *Let not the mighty man glory in his might,*
> *Let not the rich man glory in his riches,*
> *but let him who glories, glory in this,*
> *That he understands and knows me,*
> *That I am the Lord,*
> *Who practices kindness, justice, and righteousness,*
> *   in the earth,*
> *For in these things I delight,"*
> *sayeth the Lord.* (Jer. 9:22-23).

It is not enough just to know that there is a God but to know and imitate his ways, which involve kindness, justice, and righteousness.

These characteristics are all consistent with a vegetarian diet:

We work for righteousness when we eat in such a way that there is no violence toward either man or beast.

We work for justice when our diet is such that all can get their just share of God's bountiful harvests.

We show loving-kindness to all people when our diet enables them to lead a properly nourished life.

We show compassion for animals when our diet does not require their unnecessary mistreatment and slaughter.

Notes

CHAPTER 1. *A Vegetarian View of the Bible*

1. Rashi's commentary on Genesis 1:29.
2. Rabbi Meir Zlotowitz, *Bereishis*, Artscroll Tanach Series, vol. 1 (New York: Messorah Publications, 1977), pp. 75-76.
3. Sanhedrin 59b.
4. Zlotowitz, *Bereishis*, p. 76.
5. P. Pick, "The Source of Our Inspiration" (Jewish Vegetarian Society paper, London), p. 2.
6. Rabbi J. H. Hertz, *The Pentateuch and Haftorahs* (London: Soncino Press, 1958), p. 5.
7. *The Jewish Encyclopedia*, vol. 12 (New York: Ktav), p. 405.
8. Rabbi Samuel H. Dresner, *The Jewish Dietary Laws, Their Meaning for Our Time* (New York: Burning Bush Press, 1959), pp. 21-25.
9. Arlene Groner, "The Greening of Kashrut—Can Vegetarianism Become the Ultimate Dietary Law?" *The National Jewish Monthly* (April, 1976), p. 13.
10. Ibid.
11. Samson Raphael Hirsch's commentary on Genesis 9:2.
12. Dresner, *Jewish Dietary Laws*, p. 29.
13. Hertz, *Pentateuch and Haftorahs*, p. 32.
14. This speculation is considered by Pick, "The Source of Our Inspiration," p. 3.
15. For a view that God intended manna as a second vegetarian experiment, see Reverend S. Clayman, "Vegetarianism, the Ideal of the Bible," *The Jewish Vegetarian* 4 (Summer, 1967): 136-37.
16. Hertz, *Pentateuch and Haftorahs*, p. 276.
17. Talmudic sage Ben Zoma taught as follows: "Who is rich? The person who rejoices in his or her portion" (Pirke Avot 4:1).
18. Reverend A. Cohen, *The Teaching of Maimonides* (New York: Bloch Publishing Co., 1927), p. 180.

19. *Encyclopedia Judaica,* vol. 11, p. 1152.
20. Chulin 84a.
21. Pesachim 49b.
22. See the discussion in Joe Green, "Chalutzim of the Messiah—The Religious Vegetarian Concept as Expounded by Rabbi Kook" (Lecture given in Johannesburg, South Africa), p. 2.
23. Ibid., pp. 2-3.
24. Rabbi Abraham Isaac Kook, "Fragments of Light," in *Abraham Isaac Kook,* ed. and trans. Ben Zion Bokser (New York: Paulist Press, 1978), pp. 316-21.
25. Quoted in Abraham Chill, *The Commandments and Their Rationale,* p. 400.
26. Groner, "Greening of Kashrut," p. 13.
27. Ibid.
28. Rabbi Abraham Isaac Kook, *A Vision of Vegetarianism and Peace.*
29. Hertz, *Pentateuch and Haftorahs,* p. 5.
30. Green, "Chalutzim of the Messiah," p. 1.

CHAPTER 2.   Tsa'ar Ba'alei Chayim—*Judaism and Compassion for Animals*

1. Rabbi J. H. Hertz, *The Pentateuch and Haftorahs* (London: Soncino Press, 1958), p. 673.
2. Ibid.; Baba Metzia 32b; Shabbat 128b.
3. Rabbi Solomon Ganzfried, *Code of Jewish Law* (New York: Hebrew Publishing Co., 1961), book 4, chapter 191, p. 84.
4. Rabbi Samson Raphael Hirsch, *Horeb,* Dayan Dr. I. Grunfeld, trans. (London: Soncino Press, 1962), vol. 2, p. 293.
5. Choshen Mishpat 338.
6. Hirsch, *Horeb,* p. 293.
7. Rashi's commentary on Deuteronomy 25:4.
8. Hertz, *Pentateuch and Haftorahs,* p. 854.
9. William E. H. Lecky, *History of European Morals,* 3rd ed. rev. (New York: Appleton-Century-Crofts, 1903), vol. 2, p. 162.
10. Kilayim 8:2-3; Baba Metzia 90b.
11. Yoreh De'ah 297b.
12. Hirsch, *Horeb,* p. 287.
13. Gittin 62a.
14. Yerushalmi Ketuvot 4:8.
15. Orach Chayim 167:6; Berachot 40a.

16. Rashi's commentary on Exodus 23:12.

17. Hertz, *Pentateuch and Haftorahs,* p. 298.

18. Maimonides, *Guide to the Perplexed,* chapter 48, part 3.

19. Ibid.

20. Ibid.

21. Ibid.

22. Abot de R. Nathan, chapter 23.

23. Shabbat 128b.

24. Chulin 60b.

25. Avodah Zorah 18b.

26. George Horowitz, *The Spirit of Jewish Law* (New York: Central Book Co., 1963), pp. 114, 115.

27. Shabbat 128b.

28. Orach Chayim 316:2.

29. Orach Chayim 332:2.

30. Orach Chayim 332:3.

31. Orach Chayim 332:4.

32. Orach Chayim 305:19.

33. Rabbi Samuel H. Dresner, *The Jewish Dietary Laws, Their Meaning for Our Time* (New York: Burning Bush Press, 1959), pp. 27, 28.

34. Joe Green, *The Jewish Vegetarian Tradition* (Johannesburg, South Africa: Joe Green, 1969), p. 15, based on the teaching of the Ramah.

35. Dresner, *Jewish Dietary Laws,* pp. 33-34.

36. Orach Chayim 223:6.

37. Ganzfried, comp., *Code of Jewish Law,* vol. 2, p. 29.

38. Exodus Rabbah 2:2.

39. Ibid.

40. Baba Metzia 85a; Genesis Rabbah 33:3.

41. Noah J. Cohen, *Tsa'ar Ba'ale Hayim—The Prevention of Cruelty to Animals, Its Bases, Development and Legislation in Hebrew Literature* (Jerusalem: Feldheim, 1976), pp. 4-5.

42. Ibid.

43. S. Y. Agnon, *Days of Awe* (Jerusalem: Shocken, 1939.)

44. Martin Buber, *Tales of the Hasidim,* vol. 1, p. 249.

45. Ben Ami, quoted Joe Green, *The Jewish Vegetarian Tradition,* pp. 19-20.

46. A detailed treatment of how chickens are raised under factory conditions is given by Peter Singer, *Animal Liberation* (New York: Avon Books, 1975), pp. 99-103.

47. Ruth Harrison, *Animal Machines* (London: Vincent Street, 1964), pp. 54-55.

48. "Pets or Pate," *The Jewish Vegetarian* 23 (Spring, 1972): 7-8.
49. Nathaniel Altman, *Eating for Life* (Wheaton, Ill.: Theosophical Publishing House, 1977), pp. 76-77.
50. Harrison, *Animal Machines*, p. 12.
51. John Harris, "Killing for Food," in *Animals, Men, and Morals*, S. & R. Godlovitch and John Harris, eds. (New York: Taplinger Publishing Co., 1972), p. 98.

CHAPTER 3. *Preserving Health and Life*

1. Chulin 10a; Choshen Mishpat 427; Yoreh De'ah 116.
2. Pesachim 25a; Maimonides, Yad, Yesode ha Torah, p. 7.
3. Yoma 85b; Sanhedren 74a.
4. Rabbi J. H. Hertz, *The Pentateuch and Haftorahs* (London: Soncino Press, 1958), p. 843.
5. Ibid.
6. Maimonides, *Hilchot Rotze'ach*, chapter 11, part 4.
7. Fred Rosner, *Modern Medicine and Jewish Law* (New York: Bloch, 1972), p. 28.
8. Ibid.
9. Ta'anit 20b.
10. Ta'anit 11a, b.
11. Shabbat 140b.
12. Chulin 84a; Avodah Zarah 11a.
13. Shabbat 50b.
14. Leviticus Rabbah 34:3.
15. Rosner, *Modern Medicine*, p. 30.
16. Rabbi Samson Raphael Hirsch, *Horeb*, Dayan Dr. I. Grunfeld, trans. (London: Soncino Press, 1962), pp. 299-300.
17. Ibid, based on Choshen Mishpat 427 and Yoreh De'ah 116.
18. Rosner, *Modern Medicine*, p. 31.
19. Mikkel Hindhede, *American Journal of Epidemiology* 100, no. 5: 394.
20. Nathaniel Altman, *Eating for Life* (Wheaton, Ill.: Theosophical Publishing House, 1977), p. 22.
21. John A. Scharffenberg, *Problems with Meat* (Santa Barbara, Calif.: Wadsworth, 1977), p. 28.
22. Ibid.
23. R. L. Phillips, "Role of Lifestyle and Dietary Habits in Risk of Cancer among Seventh Day Adventists," *Cancer Research* 35 (November 1975): 3513.
24. Morton Mintz, "Fat Intake Increasing Cancer Risk," *Washington Post*, September 10, 1976.

25. B. Armstrong et al., "Blood Pressure in Seventh Day Adventists," *American Journal of Epidemiology* 105, no. 5 (May 1977): 444-9.

26. Ibid.

27. Gene Marine and Judith Van Allen, *Food Pollution: The Violation of Our Inner Ecology* (New York: Holt, Rinehart and Winston, 1972), p. 19.

28. Paul Dudley White, *American Heart Journal* (December 1964): 842.

29. Harold Habenicht, "The Vegetarian Advantage," *The Vegetarian Way, Proceedings of the 24th World Vegetarian Conference, Madras, India* (1977), p. 23.

30. *Journal of American Medical Association* (June 3, 1961): 806.

31. "Facts of Vegetarianism," North American Vegetarian Society Pamphlet 501 (Malaga, N.J.), p. 7.

32. W. S. Collens, "Arteriosclerotic Disease, An Anthropologic Theory," *Medical Counterpoint* (December 1969): 55.

33. "Report of Inter-Society Commission for Heart Disease Resources: Primary Prevention of the Arteriosclerotic Diseases," *Circulation* 42 (December 1970): A53-95.

34. Senate Select Committee on Nutrition and Human Needs, *Dietary Goals for the United States* (Washington, D.C.: U.S. Government Printing Office, 1977).

35. Scharffenberg, *Problems with Meat*, p. 29.

36. *Canadian Jewish News*, June 26, 1980.

37. Ernest L. Wydner, *Cancer Research* (November 1975): 3238.

38. Victor Sussman, *The Vegetarian Alternative* (Emmaus, Pa.: Rodale Press, 1978), p. 60.

39. Ibid.

40. Frey Ellis, *The Jewish Vegetarian* 35 (April 1975): 37.

41. Habenicht, "The Vegetarian Advantage," p. 27.

42. John Henry Kellogg, *The New Dietetics* (Modern Medicine Publishing Co., 1927), p. 870.

43. Dudley Giehl, *Vegetarianism: A Way of Life* (New York: Harper and Row, 1979), p. 30.

44. Habenicht, "The Vegetarian Advantage," p. 27.

45. "Facts of Vegetarianism," p. 5.

46. Ibid.

47. M. M. Bhamgara, "Yoga and Diet," *The Vegetarian Way, Proceedings of the 24th World Vegetarian Congress, Madras, India* (1977): 137.

48. Barbara Parham, *What's Wrong with Eating Meat?* (Denver, Colo.: Amanda Marga Publications, 1979), pp. 10-11.

49. R. H. Wheldon, *No Animal Food* (New York: Health Culture

Co.), p. 50, quoted by Altman, *Eating for Life,* p. 17.

50. Rachel Carson, Foreword, in Ruth Harrison, *Animal Machines* (London: Vincent Street, 1964).

51. T. Netweit, "Why Do I As a Veterinary Surgeon Prefer Vegetarian Food?," *The Jewish Vegetarian* 42 (August 1977), p. 19.

52. Habenicht, "The Vegetarian Advantage," p. 25.

53. Quoted by Parham, *What's Wrong with Eating Meat?,* pp. 15-16.

54. Netweit, "Why Do I?" pp. 18-19.

55. Karen Pryor, *Nursing Your Baby* (New York: Harper and Row, 1963), p. 65.

56. Available from the Environmental Defense Fund, 1525 18 Street, N.W., Washington, D.C. 20036.

57. Sussman, *Vegetarian Alternative,* p. 41.

CHAPTER 4.   *Feeding the Hungry*

1. Baba Batra 9a.

2. Midrash Tannaim.

3. *Passover Hagaddah.*

4. Philip Nobile and John Deedy, *The Complete Ecology Fact Book* (Garden City, N.Y.: Doubleday, 1972), p. 272. Recent reports have indicated that conditions have not improved.

5. Ibid.

6. Alan Berg, "Nutrition, Development, and Population Growth," *Population Bulletin* 29, no. 1: 23.

7. Georg Borgstrom, *The Food and People Dilemma* (Belmont, Calif.: Wadsworth, 1973), p. 63.

8. Georg Borgstrom, "Present Food Production and the World Food Crisis," paper presented on September 2, 1974.

9. *New York Times,* July 22, 1975, p. 8.

10. Quoted by Nobile and Deedy, *Complete Ecology Fact Book,* p. 277.

11. Bircat Hamazon.

12. David M. Szonyi, *Sh'ma,* (December 27, 1974).

13. Marc H. Tannenbaum, Testimony before the Ad Hoc Senate Committee Hearings on World Hunger.

14. Rabbi Emanuel Rackman, "Torah Concept of Empathic Justice Can Bring Peace," *The Jewish Week* (April 3, 1977): 19.

15. Ibid.

16. Maimonides, *Yad,* Hilchos Matnos Aniyim 7:10.

17. Ibid. 9:3a.

18. Maimonides, *Mishneh Torah,* Matnot Aniyim 10:7.

19. Exodus Rabbah, Mishpatim 31:14.

20. Pirke Avot 3:21.
21. Betza 32a.
22. Eruvim 41.
23. Nedarim 64b.
24. Gen. 18:2; Abot de Rabbi Nathan 7:17a,b.
25. Maimonides, *Yad Hazakam* Hilchot Shabbat 2:3.
26. Bezah, 32b.
27. Yebamot 79a; Numbers Rabbah 8:4.
28. Rashi's commentary on Genesis 41:50, based on Ta'anit 11a.
29. Rabbi Samson Raphael Hirsch, *Horeb,* Dayan Dr. I. Grunfeld, trans. (London: Soncino Press, 1962), vol. 1, pp. 54-55.
30. Pirke Avot 1:14.
31. Berachot 55a.
32. Paper on world hunger put out by Morzone, ad hoc Jewish group on hunger.
33. Class before *Pesach* given at Young Israel of Staten Island, attended by author.
34. Jay Dinshah, *The Vegetarian Way, Proceedings of the 24th World Vegetarian Conference, Madras, India* (1977): 34.
35. "The Energy-Food Crisis: A Challenge to Peace—A Call to Faith," a statement from the Interreligious Peace Colloquium held in Bellagio, Italy, May 1975.
36. Ronald J. Sider, *Rich Christians in an Age of Hunger* (Downers Grove, Ill.: Intervarsity Press, 1977), p. 25.
37. Boyce Rensberger, "World Food Crisis: Basic Ways of Life Face Upheaval from Chronic Shortages," *New York Times,* November 5, 1974, p. 14.
38. Lester Brown, *By Bread Alone* (New York: Praeger, 1974), p. 206.

CHAPTER 5. *Judaism, Vegetarianism, and Ecology*

1. Ecclesiastes Rabbah 7:28.
2. Jerusalem Talmud, Kiddushin 4:12, 66d.
3. Baba Batra 2:8.
4. Baba Batra 2:8-9.
5. Baba Batra 158b.
6. Barachot 30:5a,b.
7. Story told by Rabbi Shlomo Riskin in "Biblical Ecology, A Jewish View," a television documentary, directed by Mitchell Chalek and Jonathan Rosen.
8. Sefer Ha-Chinich 529.
9. Kiddushin 32a.

10. Baba Kamma 91b.

11. Berachot 52b.

12. Rabbi Samson Raphael Hirsch, *Horeb*, Dayan Dr. I. Grunfeld, trans. (London: Soncino Press, 1962), vol. 2, p. 282.

13. Ibid., p. 280.

14. Ecclesiastes Rabbah 1:18.

15. Lester R. Brown, *World without Borders* (New York: Vintage, 1972), pp. 95-96.

16. "Hunger Questionnaire" (New York: American Friends Service Committee).

17. Jon Wynne-Tyson, *Food for a Future* (London: Abacus, 1975), p. 17.

18. "World Hunger Facts" (New York: American Friends Service Committee).

19. "Facts of Vegetarianism," Publication of North American Vegetarian Society, p. 2.

20. Rabbi Adam D. Fisher, *To Deal Thy Bread to the Hungry* (New York: Union of American Hebrew Congregations, 1975), p. 3.

21. "Facts of Vegetarianism," p. 3.

22. Ibid.

23. John S. and Carol E. Steinhardt, "Energy Use in the U.S. Food System," *Science* (April 19, 1974).

24. Lester R. Brown and Gail W. Finsterbusch, *Man and His Environment: Food* (New York: Harper and Row, 1972), p. 69.

25. Frances Moore Lappe, *Diet for a Small Planet*, rev. (New York: Ballantine, 1975), p. 21.

26. Ron Litton, *Terracide* (Boston: Little, Brown, 1970), pp. 291-92.

27. "News Digest," *Vegetarian Times* (July 1980): 15.

28. Ibid.

29. Philip Pick, "The Sabbatical Year," *Tree of Life* (New York: Barnes, 1977), p. 64.

CHAPTER 6. *Judaism, Vegetarianism, and Peace*

1. Leviticus Rabbah 9:9.

2. Pirke Avot 1:12.

3. Yalkut Shimoni, Yithro 273.

4. Leviticus Rabbah 9:9.

5. Genesis Rabbah 38:6.

6. Gittin 59b; the quotation is from Proverbs 3:17.

7. Pirke Avot 5:11.

8. Rabbi Maurice Eisendrath, "Sanctions in Judaism for Peace,"

in *World Religions and World Peace,* Homer A. Jack, ed. (Boston: Beacon, 1968).

9. G. S. Arundale, "The World Crucifixion," *The Vegetarian Way, Proceedings of the 24th World Vegetarian Conference, Madras, India* (1977): 145.

10. Mark Hatfield, "World Hunger," *World Vision* 19 (February 1975): 5.

11. *Staten Island Advance,* article by Susan Fogg, July 13, 1980, p. 1.

12. Ibid.

13. Plato *Republic* 2. An historical review of the relationships among war, food production, and consumption is given by Dudley Giehl, *Vegetarianism: A Way of Life* (New York: Harper and Row, 1979), pp. 95-101.

14. The so-called "sacred cows" in India provide much work, milk, and fertilizer.

15. "When Keeping Kosher Isn't Kosher Enough," *New York Times,* September 14, 1977, p. 64.

16. *The Vegetarian Way,* p. 1.

17. Quoted by Francine Klagsburn, *Voices of Wisdom* (New York: Pantheon Books, 1980), p. 458.

18. Quoted in *The Vegetarian Way,* p. 12.

19. Quoted in *The Vegetarian Way, 19th World Vegetarian Congress* (1967).

20. Quoted by Barbara Parham, *Why Kill for Food?* (Denver, Colo.: Amanda Marga, 1979), p. 54.

21. Pandit Shiv Sharma, *The Vegetarian Way,* p. 53.

22. Quoted by Carol Adams, "The Inedible Complex: The Political Implications of Vegetarianism," *The Second Wave* (Summer/Fall, 1976): 36.

23. John S. and Carol E. Steinhart, "Energy Use in the U.S. Food System," *Science* (April 19, 1974).

24. "How Vegetarians Can Help to End World Hunger," *Vegetarian Post,* Summer 1980.

25. David Pimenthal et al., "Energy and Land Constraints," *Science* (November 21, 1975): 757.

CHAPTER 7. *Questions and Answers*

1. Pesachim 109a.

2. Baba Batra 60b.

3. Rabbi Moshe Halevi Steinberg, "A Collection of *Responsa*" (questions and answers concerning conversion and converts), *Responsum* #1, p. 2. In a recent letter, Rabbi David Rosen, chief rabbi of Ireland, points out that the argument that meat must be eaten to celebrate a holy day is refuted in the following works: (a) Kerem Shelomo (Av Bet Din of Pinzcow) on Yoreh Deah 1; (b) Yakhel Shelomo (Rabbi Shlomo Hass) on Orach Chayim 529(2); (c) Ref. Sdei Chemed (Rabbi Y. Medini), vol. 6.

4. Rabbi Abraham Isaac Kook, *A Vision of Vegetarianism and Peace.*

5. Shabbat 119; Sanhedrin 7.

6. Sanhedrin 59b.

7. Quoted by J. Green, "Chalutzim of the Messiah—The Religious Vegetarian Concept as Expounded by Rabbi Kook (Lecture given in Johannesburg, South Africa, p. 2.)

8. Ibid.

9. Rabbi Samson Raphael Hirsch's commentary on Genesis 1:29.

10. Reverend A. Cohen, *The Teaching of Maimonides* (New York: Block Publishing Co., 1927), p. 178.

11. Ibid.

12. Ibid., pp. 178-79.

13. Ibid., p. 179.

14. Rabbi J. H. Hertz, *The Pentateuch and Haftorahs* (London: Soncino Press, 1958), p. 562.

15. Ibid.

16. Ibid., p. 559.

17. Ibid., p. 562.

18. Ibid.

19. Morris Laub, "Why the Fuss over Humane Slaughter Legislation?," Joint Advisory Committee Paper, January 26, 1966, p. 1.

20. Ibid., p. 2.

21. Ibid.; Batya Bauman, "How Kosher Is Kosher Meat?," *The Reconstructionist* (April 17, 1970): 20-21.

22. Laub, "Why the Fuss?," Bauman, "How Kosher?," p. 21; Resolution of the Rabbinical Council of America, no. 16 (27th Annual National Convention, June 24-27, 1963).

23. Victor Sussman, *The Vegetarian Alternative* (Emmaus, Pa.: Rodale Press, 1978), p. 2.

24. Ibid.

25. For more detailed discussions of why vegetarians do not eat fish, see Dudley Giehl, *Vegetarianism: A Way of Life* (New York: Harper and Row, 1979), pp. 59-70, and an editorial by Philip Pick, "Is Fish All Right?," *Jewish Vegetarian* 48 (Spring 1979): 6-9.

26. J. Harris, "Killing for Food," in *Animals, Man, and Morals,* S. R. Godlovitch and John Harris, eds. (Gollancz, 1971), p. 109.

27. B. Mandelbaum, *Choose Life* (New York: Block, 1972), p. 96.

28. Shabbat 54b.

29. Shabbat 55a.

30. Tanhuma to Mishpatim.

31. Ta'anit 11a.

32. *The Jewish Vegetarian.*

33. Diana K. Appelbaum, "Vegetarian Passover Seder," *Vegetarian Times* 37 (April 1980): 44. Also, S. Strassfeld et al., *The Jewish Catalog,* p. 142.

34. Baba Batra 74a,b; Leviticus Rabbah 22:7; Sanhedrin 99a.

35. *The Jewish Encyclopedia* (New York: Ktav), vol. 8, p. 38.

36. Ibid.

37. Ibid.

38. *Josephus,* vol. 1 (Cambridge, Mass.: Loeb Classical Library, Harvard University Press, 1926), p. 7.

CHAPTER 8.   B'Tay-Avon: *Have a Hearty Appetite!*

1. Source: Anna Gordon, former dietician, Columbia-Presbyterian Medical Center, New York.

CHAPTER 9.   *Jewish Vegetarian Groups and Activities*

1. Joe Green, *The Jewish Vegetarian Tradition* (South Africa: 1969, p. 23.)

2. Philip Pick, "New Year Irresolution," editorial in *The Tree of Life,* Philip Pick, ed. (New York: A. S. Barnes, 1977), p. 20.

3. Stanley Rubens, "Reflections on a Motorway," *Jewish Vegetarian:* 45 (Summer 1978): 23.

4. Stanley Rubens, "Presidential Address," *Jewish Vegetarian:* 37 (December 1975): 16.

5. Based on the tradition of the Kabbalists, the first cup is white, the second white with some red added, the third roughly half and half, and the fourth mostly red with just a bit of white.

6. Arlene Groner, "The Greening of Kashrut—Is Vegetarianism the Ultimate Dietary Law?," *National Jewish Monthly* (April 1976): 12.

7. "Vegetarian Israel," *Jewish Vegetarian* (September 1966): 29.

8. Joseph Leftwich, Foreword, in *The Tree of Life,* Philip Pick, ed. (New York: A. S. Barnes, 1977), p. 8.

9. Information about *Amirim* was obtained from *Jewish Vegetarian* 46 (Autumn 1978): 13-15.

10. *Jewish Vegetarian* 38 (April 1976): 13.

11. Philip Pick, "The Source of Our Inspiration," Jewish Vegetarian Society Paper, p. 5.

12. *Jewish Vegetarian* 44 (Spring 1978): 43.

13. "Vegetarian Israel," *Jewish Vegetarian* 41 (April 1977): 28.

14. Ibid.

15. Ibid.

16. *Jewish Vegetarian.*

17. *Jewish Vegetarian* (Summer 1974): 24-25.

18. *Jewish Vegetarian* (Summer 1981): 18.

19. Ibid., p. 19.

20. Ibid., p. 19.

21. Ibid., p. 19.

22. Ibid., p. 20.

23. Ibid., p. 20.

CHAPTER 10. *Biographies of Famous Jewish Vegetarians*

1. Information for this chapter was obtained from the *Encyclopedia Judaica* in addition to the sources noted.

2. S. Y. Agnon, *The Bridal Canopy*, pp. 222-23.

3. Philip Pick, "Agnon, Teller of Tales," in *The Tree of Life*, Philip Pick, ed. (New York: A. S. Barnes, 1977), p. 56.

4. Joe Green, "Chalutzim of the Messiah" (Lecture given in Johannesburg, South Africa, p. 1.)

5. *Jewish Vegetarian* 39 (August 1976): 22.

6. *Jewish Vegetarian.*

7. *Jewish Vegetarian* 29 (August 1973): 42.

8. *Jewish Vegetarian* 44 (Spring 1978): 19.

9. *Jewish Vegetarian* 40 (December 1976): cover.

10. Philip Pick, "The Source of Our Inspiration," a Jewish Vegetarian Society Paper, pp. 1-5.

11. *Jewish Vegetarian* 30 (Winter 1973); 17-19.

12. *Jewish Vegetarian* 33 (Autumn 1974): 27.

13. *Jewish Vegetarian* 40 (December 1976): 14-16.

14. *Jewish Vegetarian* 51 (Winter 1979): 10; further information was obtained from a letter sent by Rabbi Rosen to the author.

15. I. B. Singer, *The Estate*, New York: Farrar, Strauss, Giroux, 1969.

16. I. B. Singer, "The Slaughter," short story in *The Seance and Other Stories*, New York: Farrar, Strauss, Giroux, 1968.

17. *Jewish Vegetarian.*
18. "When Keeping Kosher Isn't Kosher Enough," *New York Times,* September 14, 1977, p. 64.

APPENDIX

1. Pirke Avot 2:21.
2. Shabbat 118b.
3. Conclusion of *Amidah,* prayer in sabbath morning services.
4. Sabbath morning prayer.
5. Samuel T. Coleridge, "The Ancient Mariner."
6. Rabbi A. J. Heschel, *The Insecurity of Freedom* (New York: Farrar, Straus, and Giroux, 1967), p. 87.
7. Sota 14a.

Bibliography

Aleichem, Sholom. "Pity for Living Creatures." In *Some Laughter, Some Tears,* New York: G. P. Putnam's Sons, 1979.
 The great Jewish writer tells how a young boy becomes aware of the concept of *tsa'ar ba'alei chayim* (prohibition of harming living creatures) through various incidents in his life.

Altman, Nathaniel. *Eating for Life.* Wheaton, Ill.: Theosophical Publishing House, 1977.
 An excellent, concise, but very complete, analysis of all aspects of vegetarianism.

Bargan, Richard (M.D.). *The Vegetarian's Self-Defense Manual.* Wheaton, Ill.: Theosophical Publishing House, 1979.
 Thorough survey of professional literature related to vegetarian nutrition.

Barkas, Janet. *The Vegetable Passion.* New York: Scribner, 1975.
 Traces the history of vegetarianism from the biblical period to modern times.

Benjamin, Alice and Corrigan, Harriet. *Cooking with Conscience: A Book for People Concerned about World Hunger.* New York: Seabury, 1978.

 Fifty-two healthful, simple meals based on vegetarian protein, eggs, and milk.

Berman, Louis. *Vegetarianism and Jewish Tradition.* New York: Ktav, 1981.
 A comprehensive review of connections between Judaism and vegetarianism.

Brown, Lena. *Cook Book for Health* (Yiddish). New York: Jankovitz, 1931.
 An early collection of Jewish vegetarian recipes.

Cohen, Noah J. *Tsa'ar Ba'alei Hayim—The Prevention of Cruelty to Animals, Its Bases, Development, and Legislation in Hebrew Literature.* New York: Feldheim, 1979.
An excellent and extremely comprehensive survey of the laws and lore relating to animals and their treatment in the Jewish tradition. A defense of *shechitah* (ritual slaughter).

David, Nathan S., ed. *The Voice of the Vegetarian* (Yiddish). New York: Walden Press, 1952.
A collection of essays devoted to ethical vegetarian ideals.

Dinshah, Freya. *The Vegan Kitchen.* Malaga, N.J.: American Vegan Society, 1965.
A wide variety of recipes that involve no animal products.

Dresner, Rabbi Samuel H. *The Jewish Dietary Laws, Their Meaning for Our Time.* New York: Burning Bush Press, 1959.
Fine discussion of the meaning of *kashrut.* States that the ideal Jewish diet is vegetarian and permission to eat meat was a concession. Discussion of compassion for animals in Jewish tradition and *shechitah* (ritual slaughter).

Ewald, Ellen Buchman. *Recipes for a Small Planet.* New York: Ballantine Books, 1973.
Many recipes for meatless meals. Complements *Diet for a Small Planet* by Frances Moore Lappe.

Fisher, Adam D. *To Deal Thy Bread to the Hungry.* New York: Union of American Hebrew Congregations, 1975.
Excellent review of the world hunger crisis and the Jewish tradition related to food and hunger. Suggests some steps to reduce malnutrition based on Jewish values.

Frankel, Aaron H. *Thou Shalt Not Kill or The Torah of Vegetarianism.* New York: 1896.

Freedman, Rabbi Seymour E. *The Book of Kashruth—A Treasury of Kosher Facts and Frauds.* New York: Block Publishing Co., 1970.
Much interesting material on *kashrut.* A very interesting chapter on fraud in meat supervision in hotels and catering halls.

Gastwirth, Harold P. *Fraud, Corruption, and Holiness, The Controversy over the Supervision of the Jewish Dietary Practice in New York City, 1881-1940.* Port Washington, N.Y.: Kennikat Press, 1974.
An exposé of unethical practices in *kashrut,* mostly related to meat and poultry supervision, in New York City, in the period from 1881 to 1940.

Giehl, Dudley. *Vegetarianism: A Way of Life*. New York: Harper and Row, 1979.
Excellent, thorough coverage of vegetarianism. Includes discussions of world hunger, animal rights, and ecological, economic, and religious factors. Foreword by Isaac Bashevis Singer.

Godlovitch, S., Godlovitch, R., and Harris, John, eds. *Animals, Men and Morals*. Gollancz, 1971.
An excellent collection of articles on the treatment of animals, including essays on factory farming and vegetarianism.

Green, Joe. *The Jewish Vegetarian Tradition*. South Africa: 1969.
Fine discussion of many aspects in the Jewish tradition, such as compassion for animals, that point toward vegetarianism as a Jewish ideal.
_____. "Chalutzim of the Messiah—The Religious Vegetarian Concept as Expounded by Rabbi Kook" (lecture given in Johannesburg, South Africa).
Outline of some of Rabbi Kook's vegetarian teachings.

Groner, Arlene Pianko. "The Greening of Kashrut—Is Vegetarianism the Ultimate Dietary Law?" *The National Jewish Monthly* (April 1976).
Good summary of reasons why some Jews have become vegetarians.

Harrison, Ruth. *Animal Machines*. London: Vincent Street, Ltd., 1964.
Very detailed treatment of the tremendous cruelty involved in raising animals today. Shows that animals are treated like machines, not permitted any freedom or happiness.

Hirsch, Richard G. *Thy Most Precious Gift, Peace in the Jewish Tradition*. New York: Union of American Hebrew Congregations, 1974.
_____. *The Way of the Upright, A Jewish View of Economic Justice*. New York: Union of American Hebrew Congregations, 1973.

Hur, Robin. *Food Reform: Our Desperate Need*. Austin, Tx.: Heidelberg, 1975.
Very well documented study showing the many values of a nutritionally balanced vegan diet based on plant foods.

Jacobson, Michael. *Nutrition Scoreboard*. New York: Avon Books, 1975.

Jewish Vegetarian, quarterly publication of the Jewish Vegetarian Society, London, England.

Katz, Rabbi Morris Casriel. *Deception and Fraud with a Kosher Front.* Endicott, N.Y.: Midstate Litho Inc., 1968.
Fraud and deception in kosher meat-packing plants.

Kinderlehrer, Jane. *Cooking Kosher: The Natural Way.* Middle Village, N.Y.: Jonathan David Publishers, 1980.
Contains a wide variety of vegetarian recipes, many involving the use of tofu.

Kook, Rabbi Abraham Isaac. *A Vision of Vegetarianism and Peace* (Hebrew).
The vegetarian philosophy of this great Jewish leader and thinker. Rabbi Kook felt that God wanted people to be vegetarians but permitted meat as a concession, with many limitations, and that all creatures will be vegetarian in the messianic period, as they were in the Garden of Eden.

————. "Fragments of Light: A View as to the Reasons for the Commandments," in *Abraham Isaac Kook,* a collection of Rabbi Kook's works, edited and translated by Ben Zion Bokser, New York: Paulist Press, 1978.
A summary of Rav Kook's thoughts on vegetarianism. Very powerful.

Lappe, Frances Moore. *Diet for a Small Planet.* New York: Ballantine Books, 1974.
Convincingly shows the wastefulness of a meat-centered diet and that sufficient protein can be obtained from nonflesh foods.

Lappe, Frances Moore, and Joseph Collins. *Food First—Beyond the Myth of Scarcity.* Boston: Houghton Mifflin, 1977.
The real causes of widespread hunger and what can be done about it.

Leneman, Leah. *Slimming the Vegetarian Way.* England: Thorsons Publishers, 1980.
Nearly a hundred recipes to help people lose weight through a vegetarian diet.

Leonard, Blanche A., ed. *Check That Chick!* P.O. Box 5688, Santa Monica, California: Blanche A. Leonard.
"Evidence of Meat Consumption as a Cause of Cancer and Other Diseases." A compilation of extracts from books and articles that point to the consumption of meat, poultry, and fish as the prime culprit in disease.

Parham, Barbara. *What's Wrong with Eating Meat?* Denver, Colorado: Amanda Marga Publications, 1979.
Very concise and readable treatment of health, ecological, and political problems related to a meat-centered diet.

Pick, Philip, ed. *The Tree of Life, An Anthology of Articles Appearing in The Jewish Vegetarian, 1966-1974.* New York: A. S. Barnes, 1977.
A wide variety of essays on many aspects of the relationship between Judaism and vegetarianism. *Present Tense* magazine states, "Anyone who has ever felt queasy about any aspect of the meat business from the cruelty of slaughterhouses to the inefficiency of cattle as protein-sources will find much here that is thought-provoking and conscience-pricking."

Raisin, Jacob A. *Humanitarianism of the Laws of Israel—Kindness to Animals.* Jewish Tract #6, Cincinnati, Ohio: Union of American Hebrew Congregations.
Concise summary of laws in the Jewish tradition relating to kindness to animals.

Robertson, Laurel, et al. *Laurel's Kitchen: A Handbook for Vegetarian Cookery and Nutrition.* Petalema, Calif.: Nilgiri Press, 1976.
Considered by many to be the best book on vegetarian nutrition. It has 508 pages, with nearly 200 pages on nutrition, including charts, tables, etc.

Rudd, G. L. *Why Kill for Food?* Madras, India: Indian Vegetarian Congress, 1956.
Very complete and well-written case for vegetarianism, from many points of view.

Scharfenberg, John A. *Problems with Meat.* Santa Barbara, Calif.: Woodbridge Press, 1979.
Report of scientific studies indicating several health hazards associated with eating meat. Many graphs, charts, and references.

Shoshan, A. *Man and Animal* (Hebrew). Jerusalem: Shoshanim, 1963.
A very thorough treatment of Jewish literature pertaining to the Jewish attitude toward animals from ancient to modern times.

Shulman, Martha Rose. *The Vegetarian Feast.* New York: Harper and Row, 1978.
Over 200 recipes including some from India, Mexico, and the Mediterranean region. Includes menu and serving suggestions.

Singer, Isaac Bashevis. "The Slaughterer," short story, translated by
    Mirra Ginsburg.
    The Yiddish Nobel Prize winner tells of the great troubles that
    befall a Jew who becomes a slaughterer against his will.

Singer, Peter. *Animal Liberation.* New York: Avon Books, 1975.
    Powerful argument for vegetarianism. Considers cruelty to
    animals from factory farming and scientific experimentation in
    great detail.

Southey, Paul. *The Vegetarian Gourmet Cookbook.*
    Four hundred vegetarian recipes, with caloric and protein con-
    tent of each one given.

Sussman, Victor. *The Vegetarian Alternative.* Emmaus, Pa.: Rodale
    Press, 1978.
    Excellent, very complete, and well-documented case for vege-
    tarianism, with many anecdotes.

Vegetarian Thought (Yiddish). Los Angeles, Calif.: 1929-30.

Vegetarian Way, The. Vegetarianism for Health and Happiness.
    Madras, India: *Proceedings of the 24th World Vegetarian Con-
    gress,* 1977.
    Collection of excellent conference talks on such areas as health,
    nutrition, compassion, world hunger, economics, and ecology.

Vegetarian World (Yiddish). New York: 1921.

Wellford, Harrison. *Sowing the Wind.* New York: Bantam Books,
    1973.
    "A Report from Ralph Nader's Center for Study of Responsive
    Laws on Food Safety and the Chemical Harvest." Much infor-
    mation on how animals are raised in the factory farming
    system, and problems related to meat inspection.

"When Keeping Kosher Isn't Enough," *New York Times,* September
    14, 1977, page 64.
    A discussion of vegetarian attitudes and activities of American
    Jews.

Wynne-Tyson, Jon. *Food for a Future, The Ecological Priority of a
    Humane Diet.* London: Sphere Books Ltd., 1976.
    A convincing case for the adoption of vegetarianism. Covers
    ecology, world hunger, health, cruelty to animals. Also has a
    good history of vegetarianism.